AFTER MY FASHION

by Diana Morgan

SAMUEL FRENCH

Copyright © 1953 Samuel French Ltd
All Rights Reserved

AFTER MY FASHION is fully protected under the copyright laws of the British Commonwealth, including Canada, the United States of America, and all other countries of the Copyright Union. All rights, including professional and amateur stage productions, recitation, lecturing, public reading, motion picture, radio broadcasting, television, online/digital production, and the rights of translation into foreign languages are strictly reserved.

ISBN 978-0-573-13280-3

concordtheatricals.co.uk
concordtheatricals.com

FOR AMATEUR PRODUCTION ENQUIRIES

UNITED KINGDOM AND WORLD
EXCLUDING NORTH AMERICA
licensing@concordtheatricals.co.uk
020-7054-7298

Each title is subject to availability from Concord Theatricals,
depending upon country of performance.

CAUTION: Professional and amateur producers are hereby warned that *AFTER MY FASHION* is subject to a licensing fee. The purchase, renting, lending or use of this book does not constitute a licence to perform this title(s), which licence must be obtained from the appropriate agent prior to any performance. Performance of this title(s) without a licence is a violation of copyright law and may subject the producer and/or presenter of such performances to penalties. Both amateurs and professionals considering a production are strongly advised to apply to the appropriate agent before starting rehearsals, advertising, or booking a theatre. A licensing fee must be paid whether the title is presented for charity or gain and whether or not admission is charged.

This work is published by Samuel French, an imprint of Concord Theatricals Ltd.

The Professional Rights in this play are controlled by Concord Theatricals, Aldwych House, 71-91 Aldwych, London, WC2B 4HN.

No one shall make any changes in this title for the purpose of production. No part of this book may be reproduced, stored in a retrieval system, scanned, uploaded, or transmitted in any form, by any means, now known or yet to be invented, including mechanical, electronic, digital, photocopying, recording, videotaping, or otherwise, without the prior written permission of the publisher. No one shall share this title, or part of this title, to any social media or file hosting websites.

The moral right of Diana Morgan to be identified as author of this work has been asserted in accordance with Section 77 of the Copyright, Designs and Patents Act 1988.

USE OF COPYRIGHTED MUSIC

A licence issued by Concord Theatricals to perform this play does not include permission to use the incidental music specified in this publication. In the United Kingdom: Where the place of performance is already licensed by the PERFORMING RIGHT SOCIETY (PRS) a return of the music used must be made to them. If the place of performance is not so licensed then application should be made to PRS for Music (www.prsformusic.com). A separate and additional licence from PHONOGRAPHIC PERFORMANCE LTD (www.ppluk.com) may be needed whenever commercial recordings are used. Outside the United Kingdom: Please contact the appropriate music licensing authority in your territory for the rights to any incidental music.

USE OF COPYRIGHTED THIRD-PARTY MATERIALS

Licensees are solely responsible for obtaining formal written permission from copyright owners to use copyrighted third-party materials (e.g., artworks, logos) in the performance of this play and are strongly cautioned to do so. If no such permission is obtained by the licensee, then the licensee must use only original materials that the licensee owns and controls. Licensees are solely responsible and liable for clearances of all third-party copyrighted materials, and shall indemnify the copyright owners of the play(s) and their licensing agent, Concord Theatricals Ltd., against any costs, expenses, losses and liabilities arising from the use of such copyrighted third-party materials by licensees.

IMPORTANT BILLING AND CREDIT REQUIREMENTS

If you have obtained performance rights to this title, please refer to your licensing agreement for important billing and credit requirements.

To
My Husband
Robert MacDermot

AFTER MY FASHION

Produced at the Ambassadors Theatre, London, on the 8th May 1952, with the following cast of characters:

(in the order of their appearance)

JAMES TRENCHARD, a film producer	*Michael Shepley*
CHLOE GWYNNE, a screen writer	*Diana Morgan*
GEORGE PHILLIPS, a film director	*Richard Johnson*
CHRISTINE STARCROSS, daughter of Lady Starcross	*Eileen Moore*
ELLEN, a Scottish housekeeper	*Jean Stuart*
LADY STARCROSS (Mary) widow of Christian Starcross	*Sonia Dresdel*
MRS SHIPMAN (Laura) widow of Dr Shipman	*Gladys Tudor*
MRS VENNING (Alice) widow of Guy Venning	*Beatrice Kane*
MRS BENSON (Jean) formerly widow of John Halliday	*Cicely Walper*
SIBYL EMERSON, fiancée of the late Rickey Campbell	*Valerie White*

Directed by REGINALD TATE

SYNOPSIS OF SCENES

The action of the Play passes in LADY STARCROSS's *drawing-room in her home in Chiswick Mall, London*

ACT I
An afternoon in early March

ACT II
A few weeks later. Early evening

The CURTAIN *is lowered for a few minutes during the Act to denote the passing of time*

ACT III
The following morning

Time—the present

The fee for the representation of this play by amateurs is Five Guineas payable in advance to:

MESSRS SAMUEL FRENCH LTD
26 SOUTHAMPTON STREET
STRAND, LONDON, W.C.2

or their authorized agents, who, upon payment of the fee, will issue a licence for the performance to take place.

No performance may be given unless this licence has been obtained.

In the event of further performances being given, the fee for each and every representation subsequent to the first is Four Guineas. This reduction applies only in the case of the performances being consecutive and at the same theatre or hall.

The following particulars are needed for the issue of a licence:

Title of the play(s)
Name of the town
Name of the theatre or hall
Date of the performance(s)
Name and address of the applicant
Name of the Society
Amount remitted

Character costumes and wigs used in the performance of plays contained in French's Acting Edition may be obtained from Messrs CHARLES H. FOX, LTD, 184 High Holborn, London, W.C.1.

To face page 1—"After My Fashion"

[*Photograph by Houston Rogers*]

AFTER MY FASHION

ACT I

SCENE—*The drawing-room of* LADY STARCROSS'S *home in Chiswick Mall, London. An afternoon in early March.*
The room is a pleasant one on the first floor, with a window R *overlooking the river. The door is* R *of the back wall and the fireplace is* L. *The essential furniture consists of a sofa, a wing chair, a tub chair and an easy chair. There is also a small table* L *of the door, a writing-desk and chair and a small table* C.

(See the Ground Plan and Photograph of the Scene)

When the CURTAIN *rises,* JAMES TRENCHARD *is seated comfortably in the tub chair down* L. *He is a film producer, and is a dark sardonic man in the late forties, tolerant, amused and authoritative.* CHLOE GWYNNE *is seated on the sofa, glancing through a film script. She is a screen writer, and is gay, smart, very feminine, and somewhere in her thirties.* GEORGE PHILLIPS *is standing staring with moody irritation out of the window. He is a film director in his thirties. He is eager and idealistic. The three of them are obviously very much in tune with each other and very much of a team.*

TRENCHARD. Have you noticed, Chloe, that there isn't a photograph of him about the place?
CHLOE. Yes, how very odd—not even a snapshot.
PHILLIPS (*turning*) What's odd about it?
TRENCHARD. Merely that she must be a very remarkable woman. Most women with a dead hero for a husband couldn't resist a photograph of him in a magnificent silver frame on the grand piano.
CHLOE. Next to one of herself in her Presentation gown.
TRENCHARD. Or in another social milieu to one of Uncle Sid's prize vegetable marrows. (*He rises and crosses to* L *of the sofa*) Got a cigarette, Chloe? I forgot to bring any.
CHLOE. You always do, darling. And when will you remember that I'm the woman writer who doesn't smoke—and if you say I have "other vices" I'll scream the house down.
PHILLIPS (*taking a packet of cigarettes from his pocket and tossing it to Trenchard*) Here.
TRENCHARD. Thanks. Matches, Chloe? (*He takes a cigarette and tosses the packet to Phillips*)

CHLOE (*rummaging in her handbag*) Here you are—(*she hands the matches to Trenchard*) give them back—they're for the gas.

(TRENCHARD *lights his cigarette and pockets the matches*)

PHILLIPS. Jim?
TRENCHARD. Hm?
PHILLIPS. Why d'you want to make this picture? I've often meant to ask you. Prestige?
TRENCHARD. Prestige, my Aunt Fanny! The Starcross Story is honest to goodness Box Office. It's "Man's Courage and Endurance in the Face of Insuperable Odds". You can't beat it. You never could.
CHLOE. You never tried!
TRENCHARD (*ignoring Chloe, crossing and sitting in the tub chair*) I remember a writer once telling me that there were only two themes for successful screen plays—one was Cinderella and the other was the persecuted Messiah.
CHLOE. Well, as this is a bit of both it can't possibly go wrong.
PHILLIPS. What a cynical couple you are.
TRENCHARD. Cynicism is the armour of the romantic, my boy. Chloe and I are both schoolgirls at heart about this subject.
PHILLIPS. It's always been a debatable point whether Chloe has a heart at all.
CHLOE. My dear George, every time I go to the pictures and see a little boy holding a puppy and standing on the deck of a battleship with a Union Jack in the background, I burst into floods of lovely tears. What's the time?
TRENCHARD (*glancing at his wrist-watch*) Five o'clock. (*He rises and stands with his back to the fireplace*)

(*There is a silence*)

PHILLIPS. She's keeping us waiting all right.
TRENCHARD. She's entitled to.

(*There is another little silence*)

PHILLIPS. D'you think she'll let us see the famous last letter? The original, I mean?
TRENCHARD. Dunno. She's a funny woman. I only met her once with Chloe and I found her hellishly difficult to talk to. It's not going to be easy.
PHILLIPS. I suppose she doesn't really like the idea of making a picture of it.
TRENCHARD. I suppose not.
PHILLIPS (*crossing and perching himself on the right arm of the sofa*) But surely she must realize that a picture is going to be no less— no less cheap—than all those millions of stories in boys' magazines—*With Starcross in Tibet, The Last Stand of Christian Starcross*, and the rest.

TRENCHARD. Yes, but in a picture someone's got to play the part of Christian Starcross—an actor. He's got to be made up to look like him, he's got to learn to speak like him, move like him— he's got to *be* Christian Starcross.

PHILLIPS. That won't be easy for her.

TRENCHARD. No. I should think they were very much in love.

PHILLIPS. Yes. Poor woman—to have lost a man like that.

CHLOE (*gently*) He's your hero, isn't he?

PHILLIPS (*rising and crossing to the window; shamefacedly*) Ever since I was a kid.

TRENCHARD. Oh well, you're not alone in that. I found my boy playing *Starcross* with his chums only last week. They'd made the rockery the lamasery and were all set to cross the trackless wastes of the kitchen garden. There'd been that serial on the radio.

PHILLIPS. Very bad it was, too. The acting! The man who played Rickey Campbell was terrible.

CHLOE. It wasn't only the acting. The writing was atrocious.

TRENCHARD. Where do the B.B.C. find their script writers?

CHLOE. Under stones.

PHILLIPS. Who wrote it?

CHLOE. Oh, some eager young woman with flat heels from Bedford College.

TRENCHARD (*to Phillips*) I always think the camaraderie between women writers is so charming, don't you?

PHILLIPS (*grinning*) Why the hell did we have Chloe on this subject anyway?

TRENCHARD. From hunger. All the better class screen writers were working.

CHLOE (*calmly*) You know perfectly well why you hired me. A—I know my job. B—You know yours, and C—I've enough sex appeal to stimulate you but not enough to embarrass you. (*She pauses*) Is this woman never coming?

(*There is a silence*)

TRENCHARD (*sitting in the tub chair*) You realize we'll have to see all the other women, including Campbell's fiancée.

CHLOE. Sibyl Emerson? Hasn't she married?

TRENCHARD. No. Still faithful to memory. I checked up.

(*There is a silence again*)

PHILLIPS (*restlessly*) I wish she'd come. What's the time?

TRENCHARD. Two minutes *past* five.

PHILLIPS (*turning and gazing out of the window; softly*) It's just as he said in the letter, remember? "I can see the light quivering on the water, and the reflection quivering on the ceiling until the whole room is like a ship at sea—a ship in which we have made so many happy voyages."

CHLOE. I wonder if we all have that sort of last minute montage—some series of dying flashbacks? By the way, have you thought of a title? It's still on the files as *The Starcross Subject*.

PHILLIPS (*crossing above the sofa to* L *of it*) The Studio want to call it *Starcross of Tibet*, but I'm not having any. I'm not going to copy *Scott of the Antarctic*.

TRENCHARD. Or *Nanook of the North*.

PHILLIPS (*grinning*) You're just as nervous as I am—you're making cheap cracks.

TRENCHARD. What I really need is a good strong drink.

PHILLIPS (*crossing below the sofa to* R) Well, you'll have to wait for it, like everything else in this house it seems.

(CHRISTINE STARCROSS *enters. She is twentyish, with a sweet but slightly intense manner.* PHILLIPS *reacts to her appearance by staring intently at her.* TRENCHARD *rises*)

CHRISTINE (*crossing above the sofa to* L *of it*) My mother's very sorry to have kept you waiting—but she's at a committee meeting at the Boys' Home, and it must have gone on longer than she thought.

TRENCHARD. Oh, that's perfectly all right. It's Miss Starcross, isn't it? Er—I'm Jim Trenchard. I'm the producer—this is Miss Chloe Gwynne who's writing the script.

CHRISTINE (*to Chloe*) How d'you do?

CHLOE (*rising*) How d'you do?

TRENCHARD. And this is George Phillips, who is going to direct the picture.

CHRISTINE (*crossing below the sofa to* L *of Phillips*) How d'you do?

PHILLIPS (*recovering himself and thrusting out a hand*) How d'you do, Miss Starcross? (*He shakes hands with her*)

CHRISTINE (*shyly*) Do sit down.

(CHLOE *sits on the sofa at the right end.* TRENCHARD *sits in the tub chair*)

The tea won't be a minute. I'm desperate for a cup. I've been gardening.

CHLOE. It's what they call "wonderful growing weather", which means that everything comes up with a rush—weeds included.

TRENCHARD. Don't talk to me about weeds. Next year I'm going to plant weeds in my garden in the hope that the flowers will come up and choke them. (*To Christine*) Have you a big garden?

CHRISTINE. Big enough. We've got a mulberry tree which is the pride of my life—you shall have my mulberry jam for tea.

PHILLIPS. Is the famous Ellen still with you?

(CHRISTINE *looks rather surprised at his remark*)

I remember what your father said about her in his log book—

"First Ellen came to live with us, then we lived together, and now we live with Ellen".

CHRISTINE. Fancy remembering that. (*With a sudden rush of words*) You know, you're not a bit what I thought you'd be like —I imagined that all film directors wore check suits, chewed gum, and only read comic strips.

CHLOE. Oh, that type went out long ago. The new generation are all Scholars of Balliol.

CHRISTINE (*to Trenchard*) Are you?

TRENCHARD. No. I'm the generation-in-between. (*He nods at Phillips*) He is.

CHRISTINE (*to Phillips*) My father was at Balliol—oh, but I suppose you knew that.

PHILLIPS. I had his rooms.

CHRISTINE. Really? Oh, what a funny coincidence!

PHILLIPS (*smiling*) No coincidence. I fixed it.

CHRISTINE (*to Chloe*) Were you at Oxford too, Miss Gwynne?

CHLOE. No, dear, I'm practically illiterate.

CHRISTINE (*crossing below the sofa to the fireplace; slowly*) I wasn't sure about this picture. I know they made one about Captain Scott, and I know the family gave the film people every facility, but—well, it's always different in one's own case somehow. (*With another rush of words*) But if it's going to be made, I'm glad you're making it.

PHILLIPS } (*together*) { Thank you.
CHLOE } { Thank you, dear.

(*There is an awkward pause*)

CHRISTINE (*breaking it*) It's quite cold, isn't it? I must do something about this fire. (*She turns and pokes the fire*) We are always talking about leaving this house and going to a nice luxurious flat with central heating and constant hot water, but I don't suppose we ever shall.

PHILLIPS (*as if this were sacrilege*) Oh, but you couldn't!

CHRISTINE. No, I don't think we could.

(ELLEN *enters. She is an elderly Scottish housekeeper. She is pushing a tea trolley set with tea for four.* PHILLIPS *crosses to Ellen*)

ELLEN (*waving Phillips away*) I'm no so decrepit yet that I need your help, young man. (*She sets the trolley below the left end of the sofa then turns and looks at the fire*) Who's been at the fire?

CHRISTINE (*crossing and sitting on the sofa at the left end*) I have, Ellen.

ELLEN. When will you learn the difference between poking a fire and battering it to death? (*She kneels at the fireplace and tidies the hearth. Muttering*) Fires at this time of the year, too. All this soft living and loose thinking will be the ruin of the country. (*She rises*) I'll make fresh for her ladyship when she comes in.

Committee meetings at the Home indeed—just blether, blether, blether, blether. (*She crosses to the door*)

CHRISTINE. Oh, Ellen, can we have some mulberry jam?

ELLEN (*stopping at the door and turning*) Aye. My mulberry jam or your mulberry jam?

CHRISTINE (*hastily*) Oh, your mulberry jam, of course.

ELLEN. You're wise.

(ELLEN *exits.* TRENCHARD *whistles*)

TRENCHARD. Well, she may be a treasure, but she's certainly a tartar. (*To Phillips*) She put you in your place, young man.

CHRISTINE. She's like that to everyone but mother—mother can do no wrong.

PHILLIPS. Is that the Starcross Home for Boys you were speaking of?

CHRISTINE. Yes. Either mother or I have to go there pretty regularly—committees and prize-givings and things.

PHILLIPS. I gave a lecture there once.

CHRISTINE. Really?

(TRENCHARD *and* CHLOE *laugh*)

PHILLIPS. What's so funny about that?

(CHRISTINE *smiles then begins to pour the tea*)

CHRISTINE. How do you like your tea, Miss Gwynne?

CHLOE. Milk and sugar, please—and milk in last.

CHRISTINE. That's how I like it. (*She hands a cup of tea to Chloe*) Mr Phillips?

PHILLIPS. Anyhow, as long as it's wet, hot and strong.

TRENCHARD. Sounds like a publicity man's description of Errol Flynn.

CHLOE (*to Christine*) Do forgive him, Miss Starcross. He was a publicity man himself in silent film days. He used to go round followed by a bloodhound advertising *Uncle Tom's Cabin*.

TRENCHARD (*rising and crossing to the trolley; smiling*) Miss Gwynne has a lively imagination, Miss Starcross.

CHLOE. You pay me to have one.

CHRISTINE. Sugar, Mr Trenchard?

TRENCHARD. Please. (*He takes a cup of tea, crosses and sits in the tub chair*)

(*There is a pause*)

PHILLIPS (*abruptly*) Forgive me for asking you, but what's it felt like all these years—(*he crosses, stands above the trolley and picks up his cup of tea*) being the daughter of such a great man?

CHRISTINE (*picking up her cup of tea and rising*) Well, at first I was too young to take it in properly—(*she crosses below the trolley to the wing chair and sits*) I mean, I knew my father had been a very famous man, but it wasn't until I could read that I grasped it fully. Mother gave me a book called *Their Name Liveth for Evermore*. It was about people like Philip Sidney and Nelson and that boy V.C., Jack Cornwall. The last story in the book was—my father.

CHLOE. A lot for you to live up to.

CHRISTINE. Yes.

PHILLIPS. You don't remember him at all, I suppose?

CHRISTINE. No. I was only two. Sometimes I think I do, but then I know I can't possibly, and that I'm only remembering things that other people have told me. I don't even know what his voice was like, or what happened when he smiled.

PHILLIPS. You're very like him.

CHRISTINE. They say so.

PHILLIPS (*looking intently at Christine*) It's the way your eyes are set.

CHRISTINE. And my mouth, Ellen says.

PHILLIPS. Yes, your mouth . . .

(*There is a slight pause, then* ELLEN *enters. She flounces across to the trolley and deposits a dish of jam on it*)

ELLEN. Here's the jam. It's the last of the pot, but I'm not opening another for film people. You'd better keep an eye on that fire, the chimney's not drawing too well and the sweep's not due till Tuesday.

(ELLEN *turns, crosses to the door and exits. The others look at each other and laugh*)

CHRISTINE. I'm awfully sorry about that.

CHLOE. Nonsense—she's wonderful.

(*During the ensuing speeches, tea proceeds, with* PHILLIPS *passing scones and cakes to the others*)

TRENCHARD (*rising*) Can I have some more tea, please?

CHRISTINE (*rising and moving to the trolley*) Oh, do forgive me. (*She refills Trenchard's cup*) Won't you have some of Ellen's jam?

TRENCHARD. It looks galmoshy, as my son would say, but no, thank you.

CHRISTINE. How old is your son?

TRENCHARD. Thirteen. I've a daughter, too—she's ten and very, very tough.

CHRISTINE (*smiling*) Tougher than your son?

TRENCHARD. Oh, much tougher. Little girls from eight to eighteen are the toughest things in the world, bless them. (*He crosses and resumes his seat in the tub chair*)

CHRISTINE. I wish I'd been a boy—the name dies out, you now.

CHLOE. When you marry you can get your husband to change his name by deed poll.

CHRISTINE. He mightn't want to. But I must say I hate the thought of being—anyone else.

PHILLIPS. I saw the name once on a railway station in Devonshire. It was during the war and I was coming up from Plymouth in one of those trains that pause for thought every few hundred yards. It paused for half an hour's meditation at Starcross. A lonely place.

CHRISTINE. I've never been there. Mother has. They put up a plaque, you know—because of the name.

TRENCHARD. How does your mother really feel about this picture? Oh, I know she's agreed to it, but ...

CHRISTINE (*perching herself on the left arm of the sofa*) I think she's quite happy about it. She hasn't really said much. She doesn't talk about him a great deal—except, of course, when something like this occurs.

PHILLIPS. Did she like John Barclay's *Life* of him?

CHRISTINE. I think so. Again, she didn't say much.

PHILLIPS. I hated it!

CHLOE. So did I—I thought it stank!

TRENCHARD. Why? I thought he was sincere enough.

PHILLIPS (*sitting in the wing chair*) That's just what I thought he wasn't—I felt he hadn't begun to get the character of the men on the expedition. He made them flat, unreal, two-dimensional, wooden. Take Dr Shipman with that great red nose of his ...

CHRISTINE. They used to call him "Lighthouse".

PHILLIPS (*emphatically*) Lighthouse? Well, "Blackout" would have been more suitable after Barclay had done with him. And Guy Venning—now, that man was a brilliant scientist, a rare and witty companion, and Barclay makes him so incredibly dull. And Halliday, who must have had a particularly individual sense of humour and was a great archaeologist, is just a printed name on a page.

TRENCHARD (*amused at Phillips' vehemence*) What about Rickey Campbell?

PHILLIPS (*rising and standing with his back to the fire; hotly*) Rickey Campbell was turned from a daredevil into a killjoy. And rough old Dan Mowbray became a character in a minor Priestley. Here were six of the choicest spirits of this or any other age, setting out to cross the Khublai Desert—a desert never before conquered by man—and Mr Barclay writes of them as if they were a Sunday School treat on an expedition to Epping. I'm sorry I'm getting so heated, but I feel very strongly about Mr Barclay.

CHLOE. I met him once. Did I tell you? He lives in a converted mill somewhere in Essex, and in the long winter evenings reads *The New Statesman* aloud to his wife.

PHILLIPS. There you are, then. Now how could a man like that,

whose cultural horizon is obviously . . . (*He pauses for an apt comparison*)
CHLOE (*supplying it*) The Third Programme.
PHILLIPS. And whose geographic one is . . .
CHLOE. Paris with the Polytechnic.
PHILLIPS. You're too kind, Miss Gwynne. Well, anyway, how can a man like that expect to be able to write about a man like your father? A man who shone out across the drab age he lived in like an Armada beacon.
TRENCHARD (*amused*) You're very eloquent, George.
PHILLIPS. Well, let's face it, it is pretty wonderful that now and again man with his pitiful strength can throw a blazing challenge to the elements. It makes me suddenly believe in the spirit of man—almost in his divinity.
CHLOE (*dreamily*) You know, I've always wondered what the women who were left behind thought about it all. Do you remember the watchman on the *Golden Road to Samarkand* saying to the women—
"What would ye ladies? It was ever thus?
Men are unwise and curiously planned."
And a woman answering—
"They have their dreams and do not think of us."
PHILLIPS. "They have their dreams . . ." Well, Barclay's turned their dreams into suburban nightmares.

(LADY STARCROSS *is heard off speaking to Ellen*)

CHRISTINE (*rising*) That's mother. (*She crosses to the door*) Excuse me a minute, will you?
TRENCHARD. Of course.

(CHRISTINE *exits, closing the door behind her*)

Nice child.
PHILLIPS. The likeness is fantastic. (*He crosses and stands above the sofa*)
CHLOE. Repressed young woman, I should say.
TRENCHARD. Repressed and romantic.
CHLOE (*rising and crossing to the fireplace*) Not your type?
TRENCHARD. No, I'm afraid not. Give me a cigarette, George.
PHILLIPS (*taking his cigarettes from his pocket*) Oh, you like 'em to fling their girlish arms around your neck and call you "Daddy". (*He takes a cigarette from the packet and tosses the cigarette to Trenchard*)
TRENCHARD. I'm not so keen on the "Daddy" part of it. Matches, Chloe?
CHLOE. They're in your pocket.

(TRENCHARD *takes the matches from his pocket and lights his cigarette*)

PHILLIPS (*crossing to* R) That girl merely wants waking up.

CHLOE. Do you fancy yourself as her alarm clock?
PHILLIPS. My God, Chloe, you have a common mind.
CHLOE. But it's Box Office—I hope. Never mind, George, she's got a sweet little face.
PHILLIPS. She's lovely.
CHLOE. No, dear, not lovely—interesting, unusual, but not lovely. Emotionally immature for her age.
PHILLIPS. How on earth can you tell that?
CHLOE (*smugly*) Womanly intuition.

(PHILLIPS *makes an impatient gesture, turns and gazes out of the window*)

She's obviously got a terrific mystique about her father.
TRENCHARD (*rising and crossing to L of the sofa*) I think I'm glad my daughter won't have to live up to me. I don't mind betting that young woman matches up all the other men in the world against her father, and finds them lacking.
PHILLIPS (*over his shoulder*) And most of them are.
TRENCHARD. I was never one for the heights, George—give me a comfortable valley where I can look up to them and thank God my feet are on solid ground.

(PHILLIPS *wanders restlessly up* c,. *then turns and moves down* R)

CHLOE. Oh, George, do relax, dear heart.
PHILLIPS. I don't want to relax. What I want to do is to get this finally settled and done with so that I can get down to work. I've wanted to make this picture for so long—ever since I was knee high to a camera. I know that no-one but me can make it, but now it's almost here I'm scared stiff.

(LADY STARCROSS *and* CHRISTINE *enter.* LADY STARCROSS *is somewhere in the forties. She has deep eyes and a secret face. One feels that she is essentially a creature of surprises, but that her control is such that these surprises are infrequent and, therefore, when they occur are all the more startling. She is the essence of quietude, her voice is low, her hands are beautiful. She has fluidity of movement, and each time she sits one cannot imagine her in any other attitude. Her smile, which is not frequent, is singularly sweet, and her whole personality is one to which people feel sympathetic, confidential, but a triflé awestruck. When she is quiet, when she is saying nothing at all, then is her personality most felt*)

LADY STARCROSS (*moving below the right end of the sofa*) I'm so sorry to keep you waiting, but I've been half an hour late all day—I simply couldn't catch up.
TRENCHARD. I know what it's like—only I'm often weeks late instead of hours. Now let me see—you know Miss Gwynne. This is Mr Phillips.

LADY STARCROSS (*to Phillips*) How d'you do. Do sit down, everybody.

(PHILLIPS *sits in the easy chair.* CHLOE *sits in the tub chair,* TRENCHARD *sits on the sofa at the left end*)

You were filming in Italy when we had our first meeting, Mr Phillips.
PHILLIPS. Yes. I was very sorry not to be present.
CHRISTINE. Tea, Mummy?
LADY STARCROSS. No, thank you, dear, I had some at the Home. (*She sits on the sofa at the right end*)

(CHRISTINE *crosses and sits in the wing chair*)

(*To Phillips*) Whereabouts in Italy were you?
PHILLIPS. Rome most of the time. Three weeks on Capri.
LADY STARCROSS. I'm one of those people who don't like Capri —I find it sinister. And if I hadn't disliked it already that song would certainly have finished it for me! Did you have good weather?
PHILLIPS. Wonderful—and the food!
LADY STARCROSS. We ought to try being conquered and occupied sometime for the sake of our larders. Well, Miss Gwynne, how is the story getting on?
CHLOE (*rising*) I've brought the script with me for you to read. (*She crosses and hands the script to Lady Starcross*)

(LADY STARCROSS *looks at the script.* CHLOE *crosses and resumes her seat in the tub chair*)

LADY STARCROSS (*reading*) "B, sixteen. Exterior Lamasery M.C.S. Day Location. The camera pans to include Tibetan porter . . ." (*She looks up*) It looks extremely technical. I think it would be a good idea if you told Christine and me about it—how you propose to deal with it, as it were. Where do you begin?
TRENCHARD. In this room, Lady Starcross. On an afternoon like this, twenty years ago.
LADY STARCROSS. It was twenty years ago this week.
PHILLIPS. This Friday.
LADY STARCROSS (*smiling*) You know your subject, Mr Phillips.
PHILLIPS. Yes. (*He takes a deep breath*) Your husband comes in to tell you that at last he has persuaded Lord Garforth to finance the Khublai Expedition. He tells you what the Expedition means to him and how valuable it will be from the scientific and geographic standpoints. And how on his earlier reconnaissance a dying Lama had told him details of a great ruined city in the vast wastes—another Angkor. He shows you the small golden emblem the Lama had given him—the emblem that was used for currency in this dead city.
LADY STARCROSS (*smiling*) It was the golden emblem that

finally decided Lord Garforth—he was not an idealist like my husband.

PHILLIPS. He speaks of the enormous territory to be covered before they reach this city which hangs over a chasm at the foot of the Khan mountains.

LADY STARCROSS. The Tibetan porters called the Khublai *Nai tschu N'ai tang tchu*—"No End but the Edge". They thought beyond the desert lay the abyss. (*She pauses*) Go on.

PHILLIPS (*rising and moving* RC) You tell your husband that you are so pleased for his sake that his dream has come true, and he says it is not his alone. (*He pauses*)

CHLOE (*leaning forward*) Then we cut to Dr Shipman—I mean we show his house and his wife. He's told her the news and she's telling her small boy that his daddy's going on a big adventure. The child clings to his father and cries to go with him. Then we see Halliday and his wife in their garden—the Vennings in his laboratory—Mr and Mrs Mowbray locking up for the night, and Rickey Campbell and his fiancée, Sibyl Emerson, having supper at Phyllis Court.

LADY STARCROSS. I see. But is all that necessary? I mean, it is the story of the Expedition and the men who went on it—not of their wives or fiancées.

CHLOE. We want to show their domestic backgrounds, Lady Starcross, as a contrast to the tragedy that was in store for them. I think it is a permissible dramatic device.

LADY STARCROSS. But *all* of them? I can quite understand about Mrs Shipman, and Mrs Halliday—but Miss Emerson—after all, we hadn't known her very long—she was quite a newcomer into our lives.

TRENCHARD. From her photographs she looks an extremely beautiful woman—but we know, as who else should, that the camera can lie and lie. Was she beautiful?

LADY STARCROSS (*after a slight pause*) She was very handsome.

TRENCHARD. In our business, Lady Starcross, if there aren't beautiful women, we have to invent them. Miss Emerson is beautiful—(*he corrects himself*) handsome, and she exists. Therefore she is essential to us.

LADY STARCROSS. I see. Well, we can discuss that more fully another time. Please go on.

TRENCHARD. Then the preparations for the Expedition, the high hopes, the interest and enthusiasm. The dinner at Brown's Hotel, the night before they sailed. The relationship between the different individuals—how Rickey Campbell worshipped your husband, for instance. The toast they drank—"To Adventure". The good-byes' and the *Marco Polo* sailing from Cardiff at dawn.

LADY STARCROSS. She was broken up—years ago.

TRENCHARD. I know. We'll use a model.

LADY STARCROSS. And then?

(PHILLIPS *sits in the easy chair*)

TRENCHARD. Then a montage—that is, a series of shots of the journey, and then the arrival at the T'ai Ling Lamasery. We'll see the Chief Lama.

PHILLIPS. It'll be just as in your husband's log-book. (*He pauses, and then quotes gently*) "The little old man with the kind naked face sat drinking green tea and talking in excellent, if pedantic, French. He said in a tone of mixed benevolence and boredom that owing to his increasing preoccupation with Infinity, he found the desire to cross the Khublai a little perplexing."

LADY STARCROSS. Word for word!

CHRISTINE. He's amazing, isn't he?

TRENCHARD. Then they set off full of anticipation, Campbell singing *Rolling Down to Rio*—I met a man who knew him once and he said he was always singing it.

LADY STARCROSS. Yes. Poor Rickey.

TRENCHARD (*rising and moving above the sofa*) We follow them stage by stage. (*As he speaks he wanders up and down* RC) Shipman sprains his ankle and they are forced to slow down. It gets colder and colder and more and more desolate. The porters refuse to go any further, saying that the land is full of demons, and desert in a body. Venning gets a fever and they find that the porters have taken the medicine chest with them. But they have reached the point of no return. On the twentieth day, Venning dies. (*He stops abruptly and pauses. Gently*) Do you want me to go on?

LADY STARCROSS. Yes, please.

TRENCHARD (*seeing it on a screen in his mind*) Still they press forward, and a blizzard rises and blows away one of the tents. Halliday falls down a crevasse, hidden by top snow, and is killed instantly. Then one morning the sky clears and they see, miles to the north, the gleaming peaks of the Khan Mountains.

PHILLIPS. And, as if hanging in mid-air, the magic city of Tchu San Lei—"A sunny pleasure-dome with caves of ice"—*Xanadu-Shangri-la*.

TRENCHARD. The men get a little light-headed and laugh and sing. And then there is another tragedy. Mowbray falls dead in his tracks. The altitude was too much for his heart.

LADY STARCROSS. He should never have gone.

TRENCHARD. Didn't Dr Shipman examine him before they left?

LADY STARCROSS. No. Dan said his own doctor had passed him as fit. It wasn't true, of course.

TRENCHARD. The three men who are left become very close to each other. Their companionship is full of steadfastness and sacrifice. We see Shipman helping Rickey and Rickey helping Starcross and Starcross helping them both, and then the terrible night comes when the strain is too much for Shipman; his mind becomes clouded and he runs wildly away into the darkness shouting that he is pursued by demons. He never comes back. The next day Rickey begins to fail, and Starcross realizes that the end for both of them is near. They leave their last camp on a brilliant morning with the foothills of the Khans only twenty miles away. Rickey stumbles. He is carrying a rifle and it goes off. Starcross goes on alone.

PHILLIPS. "To travel hopefully is better than to arrive." The story of a magnificent failure.

(*There is a silence*)

LADY STARCROSS. Is that the end of the picture?

TRENCHARD. No. We—we would like to come back here—with Denzil Cameron and some of the rescue party bringing you the log-book and the last letter he wrote to you.

PHILLIPS. And then the award of the posthumous knighthood.

TRENCHARD. That is if you agree.

LADY STARCROSS. Yes, yes, it's all part of the story.

TRENCHARD. I think a picture like this will be an inspiration to the youngsters of today.

LADY STARCROSS. Thank you. (*To Christine*) Well, darling?

CHRISTINE. I think it will be wonderful.

LADY STARCROSS. Who would you get to play my husband?

TRENCHARD. We hope to interest some international star, but for the most part we don't want "names"—we want actors and actresses who are as like the real people as possible.

LADY STARCROSS. I suppose, from a legal point of view, you will have to get the consent of the other wives—Mrs Shipman and Mrs Venning—oh, and Mrs Halliday—she's Mrs Benson now. Gladys Mowbray died some years ago.

TRENCHARD. I'm contacting them all, now that you've been so kind. I've had an address in the South of France for Miss Emerson. She's been abroad for twenty years, I gather.

LADY STARCROSS. But surely there can be no legal necessity for consulting her?

TRENCHARD. Not a legal one, perhaps, but definitely a moral one.

LADY STARCROSS (*coldly*) I don't agree. It puts Miss Emerson in the same position as the wives of the members of the Expedition. She is not entitled to that position. (*She rises, crosses to the window and opens it, as if she suddenly found the room oppressive*)

(*The others look with some surprise at Lady Starcross. Dusk begins to fall*)

(*She turns and sees their expressions*) We all naturally hope that our friends, when they become engaged to be married, will choose partners worthy of them. We were very fond of Rickey Campbell.

He was at Rugby with my husband. He was best man at our wedding. His engagement to Miss Emerson was a bitter disappointment to all his friends.

CHRISTINE. But, Mother, I never knew—I thought . . . People said she was lovely—great fun and . . . (*She breaks off, bewildered*)

LADY STARCROSS (*gently*) There was no point in disillusioning you. A great many people found her very charming until . . . Mr Trenchard, if this picture is to be made, any contact with Miss Emerson must be avoided.

TRENCHARD. I'm most sincerely sorry, but I'm afraid it's done now. The studio cabled her yesterday morning. It's purely a matter of form, Lady Starcross—a matter of manners.

PHILLIPS (*rising*) We have to be very punctilious about things like that. All she has to do is to cable back that she agrees, and that will be the end of it.

LADY STARCROSS. I hope so. I've given my consent to this film because I believe, as you do, Mr Trenchard, that it'll be an inspiration to the young people of today, but in giving my consent I am aware that I am also giving myself a great deal of pain. Old memories, well loved faces, little incidents that looking back are almost heartbreakingly poignant. (*She pauses*) I shall be able to bear them as I have borne many things, but only if they are not cheapened or in any way soiled. Miss Emerson had a quality of cheapening anything or anyone with whom she came into contact. (*She crosses to the switch L of the door and switches on the lights*) To do her justice I do not think she did it consciously—it was just inherent in her—and I am sure that she will not have changed. (*She moves and stands above the sofa*) It is a terrible thing to say, but perhaps it was fortunate that Rickey died before he found her out. Poor Rickey, poor loyal, blind, deluded Rickey.

(*There is a silence*)

CHLOE. Forgive me, Lady Starcross, but is this opinion of Miss Emerson shared by the other wives?

LADY STARCROSS. Jean Halliday had a ridiculous schoolgirl crush on her. Mrs Shipman's and Mrs Venning's opinions I do not know. I did not discuss her with them.

CHLOE. Thank you. (*She rises*) I think we ought to be going.

TRENCHARD. Yes, we must get back to the studio. Thank you for all your kindness. By the way, I believe the studio Legal Department has sent you a letter to sign—it's just a formality.

LADY STARCROSS. It's in my room. (*She moves to the door*) I'll fetch it. I have signed it.

(LADY STARCROSS *exits*)

PHILLIPS. And we were promised some photographs.

CHRISTINE (*rising*) They're on the study table waiting for you. Ellen's packed them up. (*She crosses to the door*) I'll get them.

(CHRISTINE *exits.* PHILLIPS, TRENCHARD *and* CHLOE *stare at each other for a moment, then* PHILLIPS *makes a helpless gesture, crosses to the door and closes it*)

CHLOE (*slowly*) Now what did Sibyl Emerson do to inspire a hate like that?

PHILLIPS (*moving and standing up* R *of the sofa*) Probably turned up at the same party wearing the same hat.

CHLOE. Don't be silly, George. But I must say it intrigues me vastly. I can't wait to meet her.

TRENCHARD (*moving down* R) You won't have to wait long. I didn't tell her, but we've had a reply to the cable this morning. Sibyl Emerson is coming to England for the first time in twenty years.

(CHLOE *gives a little shudder*)

What's the matter? Cold?

CHLOE. I don't like this room.

PHILLIPS. Why on earth not? I think it's one of the most charming I've ever been in.

CHLOE. It's dead. It's as if the air doesn't circulate freely here, as if nothing had been moved for twenty years. It's like an old film set that nobody's bothered to dismantle. It's waiting somehow . . .

PHILLIPS. Darling Chloe, what nonsense you do talk.

TRENCHARD. You know, I think I rather agree with the woman for once. There is an odd atmosphere.

PHILLIPS. Don't you start getting womanly intuitions.

TRENCHARD. But there is something . . .

(*He breaks off as* ELLEN *enters. She carries a tray with a decanter of gin, a bottle of French vermouth and a decanter of sherry*)

ELLEN (*putting the tray on the table* L *of the door*) I guessed you'd be needing this. People in your line of business are born with their tongues hanging out.

(CHRISTINE *enters. She carries a large envelope containing photographs.* PHILLIPS *crosses and stands by the window*)

CHRISTINE. Here are the photographs. Thank you, Ellen.

TRENCHARD. Do you go to the pictures much, Ellen?

ELLEN (*moving to the trolley*) I do not—unless it's a Wild Western.

TRENCHARD. Ah, you're an escapist.

ELLEN (*wheeling the trolley to the door*) Begging your pardon, I'm a Presbyterian.

(ELLEN *exits with the tea trolley. The others laugh*)

CHRISTINE (*putting the photographs on the table* C) Will anyone have a drink? (*She moves to the table* L *of the door*) Gin and French? Sherry? Miss Gwynne?

CHLOE. No, thank you, dear, I don't drink.

CHRISTINE. Mr Phillips?

PHILLIPS. Gin and French, please.

CHRISTINE. Mr Trenchard?

TRENCHARD. No, thank you, I don't drink——

CHLOE ⎱ (*together*) ⎰ What?
PHILLIPS ⎰ ⎱ Since when?

TRENCHARD (*calmly*) —until opening time. (*He looks at his watch*) What luck—half past five. Gin and water, please.

(CHRISTINE *pours drinks for Trenchard and Phillips*)

CHRISTINE. Have you thought of a title for the film?

PHILLIPS (*crossing to* LC) We were talking about it earlier this afternoon—we haven't got one yet.

CHRISTINE (*handing a drink to Phillips*) What about *The Magnificent Failure?*

PHILLIPS. *The Magnificent Failure—The Magnificent Failure.* That's it! *The Magnificent Failure.*

(TRENCHARD *moves to Christine*)

CHRISTINE (*handing Trenchard a drink*) I thought of it just now —when you were telling the story—you said it was a most magnificent failure.

CHLOE. I like it.

TRENCHARD (*moving down* R) It's first class! Clever girl.

CHRISTINE (*moving and standing above the sofa*) Mr Phillips was the one who said it.

TRENCHARD. Ah, but you were the one who noticed it.

CHRISTINE. Then we're both clever.

CHLOE. Clever! You're geniuses!

TRENCHARD (*raising his glass*) To *The Magnificent Failure.*

(PHILIPS *and* TRENCHARD *drink.*
    LADY STARCROSS *enters. She carries a large envelope containing a legal document*)

LADY STARCROSS (*moving to Trenchard and holding out the envelope*) Mr Trenchard.

TRENCHARD (*taking the envelope*) Thank you, Lady Starcross. (*He takes the document from the envelope and glances at it*) I'll get this put in hand at once, and you will hear from us in a few days. (*He replaces the document in the envelope and puts it in his pocket*) Thank you more than I can say.

CHLOE (*picking up her handbag and script*) You've been sweet to us—we appreciate it very much.

TRENCHARD (*crossing to Christine*) Good-bye, Miss Starcross—thank you, too, and please thank Ellen for the mulberry jam. (*He puts his glass on the table* L *of the door*)

PHILLIPS (*crossing to Lady Starcross*) Good-bye, Lady Starcross. Thank you for making everything so easy for us. (*He picks up the photographs*) I hope we won't let you down.

LADY STARCROSS. I'm sure you won't.

TRENCHARD (*to Lady Starcross*) Oh, by the way, Miss Starcross has thought of a first class title—*The Magnificent Failure*.

CHRISTINE. Do you like it, Mummy?

LADY STARCROSS. I think it's excellent.

PHILLIPS (*putting his glass on the table* C) Splendid! That's it then, eh, Jim?

TRENCHARD. As far as I'm concerned.

CHLOE (*crossing to the door*) Even the author likes it. Good-bye.

LADY STARCROSS. Good-bye.

TRENCHARD. Good-bye.

(TRENCHARD *and* CHLOE *exit,* PHILLIPS *lingers*)

PHILLIPS. If ever you and Miss Starcross would be interested in coming down to the studios . . .

LADY STARCROSS. Thank you, but I'm afraid I'm a very busy person, Mr Phillips. However, I'm sure Christine would like it enormously.

PHILLIPS. Would you, Miss Starcross?

CHRISTINE. I'd love to come.

PHILLIPS. Good. I'll ring you if I may. (*He moves to the door*)

CHRISTINE (*moving to the door*) I'll see you out.

(PHILLIPS *and* CHRISTINE *exit.* LADY STARCROSS *crosses to the fireplace, faces it and buries her face in her arms on the mantelshelf* ELLEN *enters and stands* R *of the sofa*)

ELLEN. What's all this about a moving picture about him?

LADY STARCROSS (*turning*) It's all arranged. It's a very good thing. Part of the proceeds to go to the Home and Chair at Oxford. It's going to begin here in this room and we're all going to be in it. *All*, Ellen. They've sent Sibyl a cable.

ELLEN. Don't let her come here.

LADY STARCROSS. She's not coming here. They've only sent a cable to ask if she objects to Rickey being portrayed on the screen.

ELLEN (*bewildered*) You said it was going to start here—and we were all in it.

LADY STARCROSS (*soothingly*) It's a film, Ellen. They'll build a room like this at the studio and get actors and actresses to play the parts.

ELLEN. Well, as long as she's not coming here . . . (*She collects the two dirty glasses*)

(CHRISTINE *enters.*
ELLEN *exits and relieves her feelings by slamming the door*)

CHRISTINE (*looking after Ellen*) Temperament?
LADY STARCROSS. Not really. Just overcast with occasional showers. (*She sits in the wing chair*) I liked Mr Phillips.
CHRISTINE (*crossing to* R *of the wing chair*) They were all rather nice, I thought.
LADY STARCROSS. Yes, they were.
CHRISTINE. He had father's rooms at Oxford—Mr Phillips, I mean. I thought it was a coincidence, but he said he'd fixed it. He knows everything about him.
LADY STARCROSS. So it seems.
CHRISTINE. The way he can quote from the letter and the log-book.
LADY STARCROSS. I know.
CHRISTINE. Are you tired, darling?
LADY STARCROSS. A little.
CHRISTINE (*moving to the table* L *of the door*) Have a drink?
LADY STARCROSS. A very small one.

(CHRISTINE *pours a drink for Lady Starcross*)

Yes, I liked your Mr Phillips.
CHRISTINE. My Mr Phillips? (*She crosses to Lady Starcross, hands the drink to her, then sits on the floor at her feet*)
LADY STARCROSS. Oh, quite definitely your Mr Phillips.
CHRISTINE. Well, you shall have Mr Trenchard—he's awfully good looking and kind of reliable. I'm sure he's in great demand to be Father Christmas at children's parties.
LADY STARCROSS. He told me he was going to get in touch with the others—Laura Shipman and Jean and Alice. That means that Laura will come up to discuss it with Alice and they'll both come out here to discuss it with me, and bring Jean with them.
CHRISTINE. Do you think they'll mind?
LADY STARCROSS. I don't think so, dear. It's going to be a simple account made by obviously very sincere people.
CHRISTINE (*hesitantly*) Mother, about Sibyl . . .
LADY STARCROSS. What about her?
CHRISTINE. Was she really—what you said?
LADY STARCROSS. Darling, draw the curtains, will you—it's getting rather chilly.

(CHRISTINE *rises, crosses to the window, draws the curtains, then crosses and resumes her position on the floor in front of the fire*)

CHRISTINE. You see, even if she was the most terrible bitch, she must have loved him dreadfully, mustn't she, to hide herself away like this ever since?

LADY STARCROSS. Must she? Yes, I suppose she loved him—after her fashion.

CHRISTINE. It'll be just like twenty years ago if they all come, won't it—except for her?

LADY STARCROSS. Yes, except for her.

They sit gazing into the fire as—

the CURTAIN *falls*

ACT II

SCENE—*The same. A few weeks later. Early evening.*

When the CURTAIN *rises it is dusk but the window curtains are not yet closed. The only light comes from the table lamp on the desk and the glow of the fire.* LADY STARCROSS *is seated at the desk, writing letters. She wears a dinner gown. The telephone rings off.*

CHRISTINE (*off*) Hullo? . . . Oh yes. . . . Will you hold on a moment? I'll just ask Mummy.

(CHRISTINE *enters. She wears evening dress. She holds the telephone receiver, which is on a long lead*)

Mummy, it's Mr Trenchard. He wants to know if he can come back here after the première. He wants a word with you.

LADY STARCROSS. Oh, yes. They'll all have gone by then. Yes, that's quite all right.

CHRISTINE (*into the telephone*) Yes, Mummy says she'd love to see you. . . . Good-bye. (*She goes into the hall, replaces the receiver, then comes into the room, switches on the lights and closes the door. She brings her bag with her*) Will I do? (*She moves* R *of the sofa and displays her dress*)

LADY STARCROSS. Very nicely, except that one cheek is much pinker than the other.

CHRISTINE (*crossing to the fireplace*) Oh, bother! (*She opens her bag and attends to her make-up in the mirror on the mantelpiece*) It's because one of my dressing-table lights has fused.

LADY STARCROSS. Yes. It really is a very pretty dress.

CHRISTINE. Oughtn't I to put something in my hair? In the photographs of film premières all the women seem to be wearing nests of robins in their hair.

LADY STARCROSS. What is this film you're going to?

CHRISTINE. It's a new British picture. It's called *The Submerged Tenth*. Chloe won't go because she says it sounds as if it had a "message". And Chloe doesn't like films with "messages". (*She turns and looks at Lady Starcross*) All right now?

LADY STARCROSS. Yes, all right now. Is Mr Trenchard going to the film with you?

CHRISTINE. Not with George and I—I mean George and me. I don't think he cares for messages either. George does.

LADY STARCROSS. I think George also rather cares for Christine Starcross.

CHRISTINE (*crossing to the window*) I'm afraid he does. (*She glances out of the window*)

LADY STARCROSS. Afraid?

CHRISTINE (*turning*) Of course I like him awfully . . .

LADY STARCROSS (*smiling*) But . . .

CHRISTINE (*quickly*) But when I think of him and a man like father!

LADY STARCROSS. My dear . . .

CHRISTINE (*crossing and standing above the sofa*) Well, George is a dear and very attractive and intelligent and—and everything, but after all he's just an ordinary young man. I mean, he just wants to spend his life directing pictures. There's nothing big about him, nothing exciting. If I married George—and he wants me to—I'm afraid I should always be comparing him with father —to his disadvantage.

LADY STARCROSS. Christine, you mustn't . . .

(*The sound of a car arriving and stopping is heard off.* CHRISTINE *runs to the window and peers out*)

CHRISTINE. It's them. (*She turns*) Oh dear, I do wish I wasn't going out this evening of all evenings. I haven't seen them for so long and it is rather a special meeting, isn't it? (*She turns and looks out of the window*) Goodness, doesn't Mrs Venning look smart. What colour used her hair to be?

LADY STARCROSS. Mouse.

CHRISTINE. Well, if that's mouse I'm platinum.

LADY STARCROSS (*rising and crossing to the fireplace*) Alice has always tried valiantly, if unsuccessfully, to arrest the march of time.

(*The front door bell rings*)

CHRISTINE. I'm glad you haven't.

LADY STARCROSS. I would—if I'd the time and the money.

CHRISTINE (*crossing to Lady Starcross*) You wouldn't be anything except what you are, darling. (*She gives her an impulsive hug and kisses her*)

(*Voices are heard off*
    ELLEN *enters and stands* R *of the open doorway*)

ELLEN (*announcing*) Mrs Shipman and Mrs Venning.

(MRS SHIPMAN (Laura) *and* MRS VENNING (Alice) *enter.* MRS SHIPMAN *is pleasant and hearty with grey hair. She wears a dinner dress that has obviously seen better days.* MRS VENNING *is small, smart and discontented. Her hair is very obviously dyed and she is clinging to a youth that has passed her by some time ago. They both cross to* L *of the sofa*)

MRS SHIPMAN (*warmly embracing Lady Starcross*) Mary! How lovely.

(MRS VENNING *throws a quick appraising glance around the room*)

LADY STARCROSS. Laura, my dear.
MRS VENNING. Hullo, Christine. Not married yet?
CHRISTINE. Not yet, Mrs Venning.
MRS VENNING (*moving to Lady Starcross*) Well, Mary?
LADY STARCROSS. How nice to see you, Alice.

(MRS VENNING *and* LADY STARCROSS *peck at each other*)

MRS SHIPMAN. Christine dear, you look more like your father every time I see you.
CHRISTINE. Do I?
MRS SHIPMAN. And Ellen's not a day older.
ELLEN. Och away with you! You're no wearing so badly yourself.

(ELLEN *exits. The others laugh*)

MRS SHIPMAN (*sitting* C *of the sofa*) These shoes drive me mad. (*She eases her feet out of high-heeled shoes*) If I had to live in London I think I'd die. One morning's shopping exhausts me far more than a week's haymaking. My feet!
MRS VENNING (*turning to the fire*) I think I must get near the fire—it's horribly cold today, isn't it?
LADY STARCROSS. Christine dear, shut the window, will you? And draw the curtains. And we could all do with a drink.

(CHRISTINE *crosses to the window, closes it, then draws the curtains*)

MRS SHIPMAN. I had lunch with Alice in her flat—how she can live with that central heating!
MRS VENNING. Well, I certainly couldn't—and wouldn't—live without it.
MRS SHIPMAN. A fug, that's what it is—a fug.
MRS VENNING. Just because you like to exist in a howling draught.
MRS SHIPMAN (*laughing comfortably*) You see now why I can't get her to come and stay with me. She calls fresh air draughts.
CHRISTINE (*crossing to the table* L *of the door*) Gin or sherry, Mrs Shipman?
MRS SHIPMAN. Sherry, please.
CHRISTINE. Mrs Venning?
MRS VENNING. No, thank you.
CHRISTINE. Mummy, you'll have sherry, won't you?
LADY STARCROSS. Yes, please. (*She sits on the sofa at the left end*) Well, you both look exceedingly healthy in spite of your fugs—or your draughts.

(CHRISTINE *pours the drinks*)

MRS VENNING (*sitting in the wing chair*) I haven't been at all well actually. The doctor says I should never winter in England, but as I can't afford to do anything else I have to grin and bear it.

LADY STARCROSS. There are some charming—and cheap—little hotels in the Channel Islands.

MRS VENNING. My dear Mary, cheap little hotels are all very well for some people but not for me. I mean, can you see me in one?

LADY STARCROSS (*smiling*) Not very easily.

MRS VENNING (*eloquently*) Well!

(CHRISTINE *crosses and hands the drinks to Mrs Shipman and Lady Starcross*)

MRS SHIPMAN. The film man—Mr Trenchard—came down to see me at the cottage yesterday.

LADY STARCROSS. Oh, yes?

MRS SHIPMAN. I liked him.

MRS VENNING. Pleasant enough. I saw him this morning. I said as far as I was concerned it was all right about Guy.

MRS SHIPMAN. I sent a cable to Jack about it—but I'm sure he'll agree.

LADY STARCROSS. How is Jack?

MRS SHIPMAN. Doing very well. I have three grandchildren now and another due in August.

(MRS VENNING *shudders*)

Don't shudder, Alice—Monica likes breeding.

MRS VENNING. Really, Laura, what country life has done for you.

MRS SHIPMAN. It's done a great deal for me. At any rate I'm not afraid of calling a spade a spade.

MRS VENNING. Personally, I'm exceedingly thankful I don't have to call one anything. That's a nice dress, Christine. Leblanc, isn't it?

CHRISTINE (*crossing and sitting in the tub chair*) Yes. How clever of you to know.

MRS VENNING. Oh, I'm not quite an ignoramus. This is one of his, too.

CHRISTINE. It's lovely.

MRS VENNING. It's getting a bit tight round the waist, I'm afraid. Oh, I should have told you, Mary—I'm on a diet.

LADY STARCROSS. What on earth for?

MRS VENNING. I've put on four pounds since Christmas.

MRS SHIPMAN. And a jolly good thing, too. You look a little less like death warmed up.

LADY STARCROSS. What is the diet?

MRS VENNING. No bread, no potatoes, no sugar, no salt, no cheese, no soup, no fruit, no alcohol . . .

MRS SHIPMAN. I'd rather die!

Lady Starcross. What can you eat?
Mrs Shipman. Or drink?
Mrs Venning. Lean meat, grilled fish and salad.
Lady Starcross. Christine, run down and tell Ellen about Mrs Venning's diet and see what she can do.

(Christine *rises and crosses to the door*)

Mrs Venning. I'm so sorry I'm a nuisance, Mary.
Lady Starcross. Oh, not at all.

(Christine *exits*)

Mrs Venning. I'm glad to see you have the sense to let her dress at Leblanc's, Mary.
Lady Starcross. My dear Alice, this is likely to be her one and only. She's going to a film première tonight, so we were a little extravagant. Sure you won't have some sherry, Alice?
Mrs Venning. Quite sure, thank you.
Mrs Shipman. Jean's late.
Mrs Venning. I expect she's had another domestic crisis.
Mrs Shipman. Poor Jean, how she manages I don't know.
Mrs Venning. Manages what?
Mrs Shipman. Oh, the house and the children and the garden and everything—and no proper maid.
Mrs Venning. The children are at school, she has a gardener, a German help—I suppose you'd call that an improper maid—two daily women and a husband who likes cooking.
Mrs Shipman. What a destructive tongue you have, Alice.
Mrs Venning. It's not destructive—it's truthful. Jean's always played for sympathy. She can't do the pathetic widow stuff now she's married again, so she does the suffering housewife. If I were Bill I'd beat her, only I'm afraid that would give her the best role she's ever had.
Mrs Shipman. I'm very fond of Jean.
Mrs Venning. So am I. Only I see her as she is, not as she wants to be seen.
Lady Starcross. Don't you think it's wiser—and kinder—to see people as they want to be seen?
Mrs Venning. Not at all. I like people to be natural.
Mrs Shipman (*sharply*) Well, if it comes to that, what about your hair?
Mrs Venning (*angrily*) What about it?
Lady Starcross. Alice—Laura . . .

(Christine *enters. The tension between Mrs Venning and Mrs Shipman eases*)

Christine (*crossing to* R *of the wing chair*) Ellen says if cold ham and salad are any good . . .
Mrs Venning. Thank you.

MRS SHIPMAN. Your young man calling for you, Christine?

CHRISTINE. *A* young man is, Mrs Shipman.

MRS SHIPMAN. I went to the pictures last week—thing I rarely do. That man was in it. What's his name now? It's on the tip of my tongue. You know, the man who looks like an advertisement for toothpaste.

CHRISTINE (*crossing and sitting in the easy chair*) They all seem to look rather like that.

MRS VENNING (*to Lady Starcross*) When are they going to start this film of the Expedition?

LADY STARCROSS. Quite soon, I think.

MRS SHIPMAN. Have they seen Sibyl?

LADY STARCROSS. They've got in touch with her.

MRS VENNING. Why?

MRS SHIPMAN. Why!

MRS VENNING. Yes, why should she be consulted? She was only engaged to Rickey. Hasn't he parents or something?

MRS SHIPMAN. They're dead. And anyway, she would have been his wife.

MRS VENNING. Would she?

MRS SHIPMAN. What d'you mean?

MRS VENNING. I never thought she cared tuppence for him.

MRS SHIPMAN. She adored him.

MRS VENNING. What makes you think so? Because she does a big act and retires from this wicked world to a remote village in the South of France? Nonsense! She must have had some particularly good reason for doing it, but it wasn't because of Rickey. She was no more in love with him than I was with Guy.

MRS SHIPMAN. Alice! Really!

MRS VENNING. Well, I wasn't. Guy may have been a brilliant scientist, but he wasn't a brilliant husband—I was just an unpaid housekeeper and lab assistant to him. That's what he wanted—he didn't want a wife.

MRS SHIPMAN. My Fred always said Guy was devoted to you.

MRS VENNING. Your Fred never saw further than that nose of his.

MRS SHIPMAN. Alice, you're impossible. If I didn't know you were only speaking for effect . . .

MRS VENNING (*bitterly*) For effect!

LADY STARCROSS. You didn't say this to Mr Trenchard?

MRS VENNING. Oh, no, I was every inch a hero's widow.

LADY STARCROSS (*gently*) What's the matter, Alice?

MRS VENNING. I'm sick and tired of the whole thing. My whole life has been overshadowed by that bloody Expedition.

MRS SHIPMAN } (*together*) { Alice!
LADY STARCROSS }   { My dear!

MRS VENNING. Well, it has. Guy thought of nothing else—and since he died I've never been able to get away from it. I lived with his parents as you know till they died—I was made to feel that it was my duty. When any other man was attracted to me, old Mrs Venning used to tell them that my heart was buried in Tibet, and after a time they all sheered off. Oh, I don't deny I enjoyed playing a woman dedicated to the dead for several years, but the enjoyment wore off, and I woke up and found myself a lonely, middle-aged woman with a service flat and a bitter tongue. (*She rises and moves to the fireplace*) A lonely middle-aged woman with dyed hair clinging to a departed youth because she had nothing else to cling to.

LADY STARCROSS. Alice, my dear . . .

MRS VENNING. And what good did that Expedition do? That's what I want to know.

CHRISTINE. What good?

MRS SHIPMAN. Really, of all the fantastic . . .

MRS VENNING. Yes, what good? Did it further science?

CHRISTINE. Of course it did.

MRS VENNING. Rubbish! All they left were a few meteorological reports and some notes on minerals and flora and fauna. They didn't even reach the city. In fact that Expedition didn't do a thing but lose six men's lives and Lord Garforth's money.

CHRISTINE. Mrs Venning!

MRS VENNING. If I've shocked you, Christine, I'm sorry, but there it is.

CHRISTINE. But, Mrs Venning, the Expedition has been an inspiration to millions—that's why they're making the film.

MRS SHIPMAN. The trouble with you, Alice, is that you sit in that stuffy flat day after day letting your imagination run riot, and getting thoroughly morbid. What good did the Expedition do? Do you think men like my Fred and Dan Mowbray would have gone on if it wasn't going to do good?

MRS VENNING. They'd have done far more good if they'd stayed at home and looked after their jobs and their families. Fred was a good doctor—think of the lives he lost in losing his.

MRS SHIPMAN. Be quiet, Alice.

MRS VENNING. Look what it's done to all of you, too. You, Laura, have come out of it best, but then you're one of those lucky people who believe that Allah is Great and Britannia is his Prophet—you're fortunate that you haven't got an imagination to run riot. Jean's married again, but I don't envy Bill Benson. Everywhere they go sooner or later she lets drop the fact that she was married to John Halliday. Bill got very drunk one evening and let down his back hair to me—he said it was a rotten business sharing his wife with a damned ghost.

LADY STARCROSS. Please, Alice, that's enough.

MRS VENNING. And you, Mary. You've become a monument to the Expedition. You're not a woman any longer—you're a granite figure carrying a granite torch. And there's one thing more—if they'd all come back successfully it would just have been another Expedition. But because they died, and because they failed, they became heroes.

CHRISTINE. How dare you!

MRS VENNING. If Christian had crossed the desert and come safe home he'd have been no legend!

MRS SHIPMAN. Stop that blasphemous nonsense, you—you wicked woman!

LADY STARCROSS (*rising and crossing to Mrs Venning*) Oh, Alice—my poor Alice, have you really been thinking like this all these years? Everything you say is false, false.

(ELLEN *enters and stands in the open doorway. Her customary calm has deserted her*)

ELLEN (*announcing*) Mrs Benson and . . .

(MRS BENSON (Jean) *bustles into the room. She is good-hearted, tactless and rather silly*)

MRS BENSON. My dears—look who I've brought with me.

(SIBYL EMERSON *enters. She is a dark woman with a strange and arresting beauty and a strange and individual voice. She is a very vivid personality and it is impossible to be indifferent to her either way. There is a faintly mocking edge to her smile. She wears a perfectly cut dark suit and carries a coat.*
    ELLEN *exits, closing the door behind her.* LADY STARCROSS *stares at Sibyl.* MRS SHIPMAN *rises and turns*)

It's Sibyl!

MRS SHIPMAN. Sibyl—my dear.

MRS VENNING. Sibyl!

SIBYL (*moving below the right end of the sofa*) Yes, it's me.

MRS BENSON (*crossing and standing above the left end of the sofa; excitedly*) I was just on the point of leaving the house when the phone rang, and when I answered it was her!

SIBYL (*to Lady Starcross*) I'm not a ghost, Mary.

LADY STARCROSS. You've not changed.

MRS SHIPMAN (*moving to Sibyl and kissing her*) It's good to see you, Sibyl—we've missed you all these years.

SIBYL. It's good to see you, Laura. And Alice. Everybody looks exactly the same. I suppose it's because we're the same generation and age in step with each other. (*She turns and sees Christine*) You're Christine.

(CHRISTINE *rises*)

(*She crosses to* L *of Christine*) I'd know you anywhere.

MRS SHIPMAN. The likeness is extraordinary, isn't it?

LADY STARCROSS. We'd no idea you were in London. Do sit down. (*She sits in the tub chair*)

(MRS SHIPMAN *sits on the sofa at the left end*. MRS VENNING *sits in the wing chair*. SIBYL *crosses and sits on the sofa at the right end*. MRS BENSON *crosses and sits in the easy chair*. CHRISTINE *stands above the easy chair*)

SIBYL. I had a letter from Mr Trenchard about the film so I came over. I saw him and his director this morning. I'd been wanting to come back for some time and this seemed a good reason for coming.
LADY STARCROSS. You'll stay for dinner, I hope?
SIBYL. Thank you—I'd love to.
MRS VENNING. Have you left France for good?
SIBYL. No, I've dug in my roots too deep. D'you know it's twenty years since I was in London?
CHRISTINE. Do you find it very much changed?
SIBYL. It's greyer and shabbier, more damaged than I'd imagined, but it still has more magic for me than any other city.
MRS SHIPMAN. What happened to you in the war? I was so worried about you.
SIBYL. I was in the unoccupied part. I worked in a hospital.
MRS BENSON. She'd no idea I'd married again—she'd no idea we were alive. She just rang up my old number and the Lawsons who are still there gave her my new one. I was in the middle of the most fearful domestic crisis——

(MRS VENNING *looks pointedly at Mrs Shipman*)

—but I just dropped everything, literally, and rushed round to the hotel.
LADY STARCROSS (*nodding towards the table* L *of the door*) Sherry, Christine.

(CHRISTINE *crosses to the table* L *of the door and pours two glasses of sherry*)

MRS VENNING. Not *another* domestic crisis, Jean?
MRS BENSON. Oh yes, it was terrible. Bill was out—and my German was sulking in her room, and one of the daily women had toothache and on top of all this, Sibyl's voice. You know, she didn't know I'd two children or anything!

(CHRISTINE *moves to Sibyl and hands her a drink*)

SIBYL (*smiling*) Perhaps I am a ghost after all.
MRS SHIPMAN. A very nice one.
MRS VENNING. A very smart one.
SIBYL. You're very smart yourself, Alice—but then you always were. Where are you living now?
MRS SHIPMAN. She's in a pressure cooker off Sloane Street.

SIBYL. And where are you, Laura?
MRS VENNING. She's in a refrigerator in Essex.

(CHRISTINE *moves to Mrs Benson and hands her a drink*)

MRS BENSON. My dear, what an enormous sherry. I shall be quite tiddly.
SIBYL. This room's just the same—no, the curtains are new.
MRS BENSON. Mary's taken the portrait of Christian upstairs. (*She points to the fireplace*) It used to be over there—remember?
SIBYL. Yes. Yes, so it was.

(ELLEN *enters*)

ELLEN (*to Christine*) That Mr Phillips is downstairs. He's waiting for you.
MRS VENNING. The film man?
CHRISTINE. Yes, he's taking me to a première. Good-bye, everybody. Good-bye, Mummy. I do wish I wasn't going.
LADY STARCROSS. Run along, dear.
MRS SHIPMAN. Have a lovely time.
CHRISTINE. Thank you.
MRS BENSON. Good-bye—you look simply lovely.
MRS VENNING. Good-bye.
SIBYL. Good-bye.

(CHRISTINE *exits*. ELLEN *follows her off*)

She's a darling—you're lucky, Mary.
MRS BENSON. She's so like Christian. Wait till you see my Jennifer though, Sibyl. Bill says everybody will be taking her for my sister in a few years.
MRS SHIPMAN. How old is she?
MRS BENSON. Twelve, but she looks more.
MRS VENNING. Is she still as fat as she was?
MRS BENSON. I prefer a plump kiddie to a skinny one—actually it took me years to lose my puppy fat and Jennifer's the same. I can't wait for you to see her, Sybil.
MRS SHIPMAN (*to Sybil*) Now you're not going to let another twenty years go by without seeing us. You must promise that. Where are you staying?
SIBYL. Durrant's Hotel. I tried Garland's but it wasn't there. I think that upset me more than anything. We'd always stayed there when I was a child, you know.
MRS SHIPMAN. Are you still working in a hospital?
SIBYL. No, I gave that up four years ago.
MRS SHIPMAN. What do you do with yourself all the time?
MRS VENNING. She's very social I should think—aren't you, Sibyl?
SIBYL. Not in the accepted sense—we're very unfashionable at Valcassier. It's just a little village—the nearest market town is

twenty kilometres away and the buses only run three days a week. No, I garden, I read, I do the marketing, I give the curé English lessons—things like that.

MRS BENSON. Are there any nice people about—I mean—you know, people you can be friends with?

MRS VENNING. Jean means English people.

SIBYL. No, no English people.

MRS BENSON. I can't imagine how you can bear it, can you, Mary? (*To Sibyl*) Aren't you lonely?

SIBYL. No, not out there. I feel very lonely in London, though.

MRS BENSON. Well, that's entirely your own fault—you should have let us know you were coming. We'd have met you and . . .

MRS SHIPMAN. You must come to the cottage for the weekend.

MRS VENNING. If you don't mind about catching pneumonia . . .

MRS BENSON (*rising and crossing to the table* L *of the door*) Talking about pneumonia, my dear, I've been so worried about Frankie. (*She puts her glass on the table*) You know, these school matrons really are impossible. She's been letting him wear his sleeveless pullover in this weather.

LADY STARCROSS. Do help yourself to another sherry, Jean.

MRS BENSON. Oh, thanks. (*She refills her glass*) I had to write to the headmaster and complain, and I simply hate having to do that, don't you?

MRS VENNING. I've never had to do it.

MRS BENSON (*perching himself on the left arm of the sofa*) You don't know how lucky you are, all of you, with simply no domestic worries. My goodness, I envy you! And fancy living in the South of France like Sibyl. . . .

MRS VENNING (*abruptly*) I've never been able to understand it.

MRS BENSON. What?

MRS VENNING. Sibyl of all people burying herself in a French village—not even on the Riviera—for twenty years. (*To Sibyl*) You with your looks and your money and—and your intelligence —wasting yourself.

SIBYL. I'm very content, Alice.

MRS VENNING. And living by yourself—if you *do* live by yourself.

SIBYL. I've a cook and a gardener.

MRS VENNING. Oh, you know what I mean.

SIBYL. I haven't any lover, if that's what you mean.

MRS VENNING. Well, I don't understand it—I really don't.

MRS BENSON. It seems quite ridiculous that I should have had two husbands while . . .

SIBYL. While I haven't had one?

MRS BENSON. Well, yes. It's so absurd to think of you as a spinster.

MRS VENNING. I notice you don't say as a virgin.

Mrs Shipman. Alice!

Mrs Benson. Really, Alice!

Sibyl (*smiling*) Well, that was what you meant, wasn't it, Jeannie?

Mrs Benson (*flustered*) Of course it wasn't. Alice is always so—so basic. What I meant was that you didn't look as if you hadn't —as if you weren't . . .

(Mrs Venning *laughs*)

Don't laugh like that, Alice. (*She rises and crosses to* RC)

Mrs Venning. What do you think, Mary—do you think Sibyl looks like a—spinster?

Lady Starcross. I think Sibyl looks very well.

Mrs Shipman. She looks a jolly sight better than you do, Alice, but that's because she's got some good fresh air into her lungs.

Mrs Venning. I wasn't talking about her health.

Mrs Shipman. Well, I was. I haven't got sex on the brain like you town folk with all your picture-houses, bridge clubs and lending libraries—and I don't care if Sibyl looks like a tart as long as she looks well.

Mrs Venning. What do you simple country folk know about tarts?

Sibyl. All tarts were simple country girls once, Alice.

Mrs Shipman. Sibyl!

(Sibyl *laughs, rises and crosses to* R *of the wing chair*)

Sibyl. Oh, darlings, it is nice to see you again. Dear Laura. (*She holds Mrs Shipman's hand and pats it*) I've missed you very much—and Alice—yes, I have, Alice. And Jeanie.

Mrs Benson. And Mary.

Sibyl. Of course.

Mrs Benson. And to think that we shall all be characters in a film.

Sibyl (*to Lady Starcross*) Are you going to let them make this film, Mary?

Lady Starcross. Certainly—why not?

Sibyl. I can't tell you how strongly I feel that it shouldn't be made.

Lady Starcross. For what reason?

Sibyl. Oh, I haven't a proper reason. It's a feeling, an instinct, rather than a reason. Can you face seeing actors being—them?

Mrs Venning. You needn't see the picture, Sibyl—you're under no compulsion to do so.

Sibyl (*crossing above the sofa to* R) It's all so false. All done with mirrors, models and Max Factor.

Mrs Shipman. But there've been films about everybody—why,

Queen Victoria was in *Annie Get Your Gun*. I must say I was very surprised, but there she was.

MRS BENSON. In technicolor, too. (*She sits on the sofa at the right end*)

SIBYL. I don't think I realized—living where I do—quite how world famous the whole thing had become—how it had grown and become history.

MRS SHIPMAN. Does that upset you?

SIBYL. It seems out of proportion somehow.

LADY STARCROSS. How?

SIBYL. Oh, Mary, I can't explain.

LADY STARCROSS. I think you must.

SIBYL. I'll try. (*She moves restlessly to the window, then turns*) It's as if you had a small but very lovely house—perfect proportions, simple, exquisite—and you left it and went away for many years. During your exile you heard rumours of how it was being altered and improved, and then you suddenly learnt that a whole new wing was to be added and you were worried and hurried home. And you found your simple little house had become a gorgeous palace with pinnacles and turrets and swimming pools and the public paid two and sixpence to be shown over it every Wednesday. It wasn't your house any more—it was a public outing.

LADY STARCROSS. I see. You would rather keep the house small and empty than enlarge it and give happiness to others?

SIBYL. You make me sound very selfish.

LADY STARCROSS (*gently*) You *are* selfish, Sibyl. I have always thought of you as the most selfish woman I have ever known.

MRS BENSON. Mary!

LADY STARCROSS. Only a selfish woman would have disappeared as you did. The rest of us had to go on and face the world. Laura and I had children to bring up, Alice had Guy's parents to look after. Jean had no money and had to take a job. But you—you wrapped yourself in the mantle of heartbreak and departed for the South of France. You helped nobody.

MRS BENSON. But, Mary—she was terribly unhappy—Rickey was her life.

LADY STARCROSS. Do you think Christian wasn't mine?

SIBYL (*sitting in the easy chair*) I'm sorry. I shouldn't have come.

LADY STARCROSS. But you *have* come. You've come and you've tried to make us feel that in agreeing to this film we were cheapening our dead husbands.

SIBYL. I didn't mean to make you feel like that.

LADY STARCROSS. For twenty years we've lived with the glory of their achievement—and that glory has grown, and is still growing. Christian Starcross is a name that will last as long as humanity exists. (*She rises*) Don't think that you can do anything to lessen its fame.

SIBYL (*rising*) I am not thinking of lessening its fame—only of limiting it.

LADY STARCROSS. Limiting it?

SIBYL. Yes, I'm so very frightened.

MRS SHIPMAN. My dear Sibyl.

SIBYL. What's the Greek word—*hubris*—yes, that's what I'm frightened of. I'm frightened of defying the Gods.

MRS SHIPMAN. How are you "defying the Gods"?

SIBYL. You see, I didn't realize what had happened . . .

LADY STARCROSS. What are you trying to say, Sibyl?

SIBYL (*urgently*) Don't let this picture be made, Mary. You can stop it. I entreat you not to let it be made.

LADY STARCROSS (*crossing to Sibyl*) A large proportion of the proceeds are to go to the Starcross Homes and the Chair at Oxford. Would you stop that?

SIBYL. I've got money—too much money, they can have it all.

MRS SHIPMAN. You're talking nonsense!

MRS VENNING. If they took it all that's the end of the South of France for you.

SIBYL. Oh, you all talk as if the South of France was all glitter and glamour. I don't lead that sort of life—I've told you. If the Homes and the Chair at Oxford need money I can give it to them instead.

LADY STARCROSS. You can give it as well. This film is going to be made, Sibyl.

SIBYL. No, Mary.

(LADY STARCROSS *and* SIBYL *hold each other's eyes, unaware of anyone or anything except their own inflexible determinations. There is a short silence.*

ELLEN *enters. The tension eases*)

ELLEN. Dinner is served.

MRS SHIPMAN (*rising; with heartfelt relief*) Thank God!

The CURTAIN *falls for a few minutes to denote the passing of time.*

When the CURTAIN *rises again, dinner is over and coffee is being served. The trolley is set below the sofa and* LADY STARCROSS *stands R of it.* MRS VENNING *is seated in the tub chair.* MRS BENSON *is standing above the right end of the sofa with her cup and saucer in her hand.* MRS SHIPMAN *is seated in the wing chair.* SIBYL *is standing gazing out of the window, smoking a cigarette. There is a babble of talk.*

MRS BENSON. . . . and I said to Bill—oh dear, I've forgotten what I did say to him.

LADY STARCROSS. More coffee, Alice?

MRS VENNING. No, thank you.

LADY STARCROSS. Sibyl?

(SIBYL *shakes her head*)

What about you, Jean?

MRS BENSON. I'd adore some. My goodness, I'm quite tight.

LADY STARCROSS. Nonsense! (*She takes Mrs Benson's cup*)

MRS BENSON. But I am. I always remember darling John saying the night before he sailed, "Kitten, you're sozzled", and I was. I've simply no head for drink at all.

LADY STARCROSS (*filling Mrs Benson's cup*) Then you'd better have it black. Here you are. (*She hands the cup to Mrs Benson*) Sure you don't want to change your mind, anybody? Alice?

MRS VENNING. Coffee keeps me awake, I'm afraid.

(LADY STARCROSS *moves* R *of the sofa, then above it to* C)

Besides, I'm only allowed four cups of liquid a day—I'm being dehydrated.

MRS SHIPMAN (*rising*) I must say it sounds the most utter rubbish to me. I always thought that the way to slim was to drink plenty of water and flush your kidneys.

MRS BENSON. Oh, Laura, how disgusting.

MRS VENNING. That's the way to waterlog your system completely. Now my Dr Hopkins . . .

MRS BENSON (*interrupting*) Oh, you and your Dr Hopkins!

SYBIL (*turning sharply*) Please, can't we get back to the film?

MRS VENNING. There doesn't seem much point, does there? I mean, you say one thing and Mary says another and there we are. Besides, it's late and I've got to get up early in the morning. (*She rises*)

MRS SHIPMAN. What do you call early?

MRS VENNING. I've got to be out by half past ten at the latest.

MRS SHIPMAN. My God!

MRS BENSON. Really, Laura, your language.

MRS SHIPMAN. I've got to be out at six o'clock all the year round, rain or shine. Some people don't know they're born. (*She crosses to Lady Starcross*) Well, Mary dear, we've had a lovely evening—and don't forget that you and Christine are coming down in June.

LADY STARCROSS. Thank you, Laura, we'd love to.

MRS BENSON. I suppose I'll be able to drive. If I'm too squiffy you'll have to take over from me, Sibyl. (*She puts her cup on the trolley*)

SIBYL. I won't be coming with you, Jeanie, I'm afraid. I'm going to ask Mary if I can stay behind and talk to her for a few moments.

LADY STARCROSS. Oh?

MRS BENSON (*plumping down on the sofa*) Oh, well, I suppose I'd better wait for you.

SIBYL. No, Jeanie—please.

MRS BENSON (*rising; slightly offended*) Oh, very well then. (*She moves up* RC) Good night, Mary, and thank you.

Mrs Venning (*crossing below the sofa to* c) Good night, Mary. I'll ring you up next week and we'll lunch.
Mrs Shipman (*crossing to the door*) You mean Mary'll lunch. Good night, Sibyl, my dear, I'll ring you in the morning.
Sibyl. Bless you, Laura.
Mrs Benson (*to Sibyl*) Don't forget you're coming to us to-morrow evening.
Sibyl. I won't.
Mrs Benson (*moving to the door*) If I crash into a lamp-post I'll tell the police it was your fault for not coming with me.
Mrs Shipman. Come on, Jean—you're not as bad as you think.
Mrs Venning. Good night, Sibyl. Nice to have seen you. I'm in the book. Coming, Laura?
Lady Starcross. I'll come down with you.
Mrs Shipman. You'll do nothing of the sort—we ought to know our way by this time. Good-bye. Thank you.
Lady Starcross. Good-bye, Laura dear.

(Mrs Shipman *exits*. Mrs Benson, *giggling, follows her off*)

Mrs Venning (*moving to the door*) Good-bye.
Lady Starcross }
Sibyl } (*together*) Good-bye.

(Mrs Venning *exits*)

Sibyl. Jean's all right, isn't she?
Lady Starcross (*closing the door*) Perfectly, but she enjoys pretending she might not be.
Sibyl. Mary, now that they've gone, let me entreat you . . .
Lady Starcross (*interrupting gently*) I'm going to ring for Ellen to take the coffee things out first. (*She crosses to the fireplace and presses the bell-push*)

(Sibyl *gives a hopeless gesture and turns to the window*)

I'm glad you're going to Jean's tomorrow. You'll like Bill. He's got a particularly nice smile. It lasts at the corners of his mouth long after his eyes are grave. They're very happy.
Sibyl (*turning*) Alice looked miserable, I thought.
Lady Starcross. The world has always owed Alice a living and she has done nothing to earn her salary.
Sibyl. Poor Alice.
Lady Starcross. I believe you get out of life what you put into it. Alice has put nothing.
Sibyl. Some of us haven't much to put, you know.

(Ellen *enters*)

ELLEN (*glaring at Sibyl; sharply*) Oh, you're still here.

(*The hostility in Ellen's voice puzzles* SIBYL, *who looks at Lady Starcross in surprise*)

LADY STARCROSS. Miss Emerson wanted to talk to me alone, Ellen. You may clear.

ELLEN (*crossing to the trolley*) She's no trying to . . .

LADY STARCROSS (*interrupting firmly*) You may clear, Ellen.

(*For a moment it looks as if* ELLEN *were going to disobey, but she wheels the trolley to the door*)

SIBYL. What's the matter, Ellen? We used to be such friends.
ELLEN. You were no friend to anyone in this house.

(ELLEN *exits with the trolley, closing the door behind her*)

SIBYL. What did she mean?
LADY STARCROSS. She's old. She's prejudiced. Perhaps she thinks life's been too easy for you.
SIBYL. As you do?
LADY STARCROSS. As I do.
SIBYL. My life ended twenty years ago.
LADY STARCROSS. Only yours?
SIBYL. Oh, Mary, if I seem selfish—well, try to forgive me.
LADY STARCROSS (*moving to the desk*) For being as you are? (*She takes some embroidery from the desk drawer and moves below the sofa*)
SIBYL (*slowly*) You used not to dislike me like this, Mary—neither you nor Ellen.

(*There is silence, during which* LADY STARCROSS *sits on the sofa and begins to work on the embroidery*)

LADY STARCROSS (*presently*) I suppose you're going to give me your reason why you're against the film being made.
SIBYL. No—I've not got a reason to give. I'm going to entreat you, Mary, for everyone's sake—for Christian's sake.
LADY STARCROSS. It's no good, Sibyl.
SIBYL. But, Mary, I came specially to . . .
LADY STARCROSS. I can't help that—it's no good, Sibyl.
SIBYL. You're determined?
LADY STARCROSS. Quite determined.
SIBYL (*crossing above the sofa to the fireplace*) If entreaties won't work there are threats.
LADY STARCROSS (*faintly amused*) You would threaten—me?
SIBYL. Lord Garforth's paper is still the most powerful in the country and they would publish what I wrote.
LADY STARCROSS. What would you write?
SIBYL. The film industry is a young one and like all young things is rather unsure of itself and always afraid of making errors of taste—and of putting the public against itself. I could write

and say how mostrous it was for living women to see the men they had loved on a flickering screen in the Edgware Road.

Lady Starcross. From what angle would you write it—as Rickey's fiancée or as Christian's mistress?

(*There is a silence as* Sibyl, *thunderstruck, stares at Lady Starcross*)

(*Intent on her work*) Did you think I didn't know? I remember the first time you came here. It was a summer evening and we were having a little party. I was wearing a blue dress—Christian always liked me in blue. Rickey rang up and asked if he could bring his fiancée to meet us. Christian said, "What d'you bet she's small and fluffy and dumb as hell?" And then you came. You were very quiet, very demure and your eyes fluttered. I saw you looking round the room and you said to me, "Oh, Mrs Starcross, what a perfectly lovely room. I want everything you've got." I didn't realize then that Christian went with the furniture.

Sibyl (*crossing and sitting* L *of Lady Starcross on the sofa*) Oh, Mary, forgive me. I couldn't help it. When Rickey said, "This is Christian", I knew. It was like coming home.

Lady Starcross (*looking up*) He was my husband.

Sibyl. Mary, I'm so desperately sorry—not for loving Christian but that you knew—that you were hurt.

Lady Starcross. You're not sorry that you deceived me?

Sibyl. No. Only that you were not more deceived.

Lady Starcross. You're honest in that, at least.

Sibyl. I try to be honest.

Lady Starcross. And is it honest to steal another woman's husband?

Sibyl (*rising and crossing to the fireplace*) I never thought of Christian as anyone's husband. He was just—Christian. I never have been able to think of people as belonging to other people.

Lady Starcross. The prisons are full of individuals with that particular attitude towards other people's property.

Sibyl. Mary, I was speaking of men and women, not of things. I didn't steal Christian from you—I only took that part of him that was mine by rights.

(Lady Starcross *gives a bitter little laugh*)

Lady Starcross. "Rights"—you talk to me of "rights".

Sibyl (*crossing and sitting* L *of Lady Starcross on the sofa*) Oh, Mary—Mary dear, please try to understand. I took nothing from you. You had Christian's home, his career, his child, his love for you. Did you lose any of those because he gave another love to me? The love he gave me was the love I inspired in him, the love that was waiting for me till I came. All my life I'd been lonely—looking for something, for someone. Oh, I know I "had everything" as they say—youth, money, looks, Rickey. . . . But I was like a house with a dark corner that cast its shadow wherever you walked. And Christian came and threw out a window to the sun.

LADY STARCROSS. Did you never think of what you were doing to me?

SIBYL. Where is your honesty, Mary? I never touched you. Christian was happier with you than ever before because he was so happy with me. He would let nothing affect his life with you—oh, I'd get hysterical and beg him to leave you and let me break with Rickey, but it was no use. He wanted you and his home in Chiswick and me and my flat in Chelsea. He needed both of us to complete him—some men are like that—most men are like that.

LADY STARCROSS. And were you to go on sleeping with Christian after your marriage to Rickey?

SIBYL (*rising and crossing to the fireplace*) Oh, Mary, you make it all sound so sordid.

LADY STARCROSS. It *was* sordid. Sordid and untidy. (*She neatly folds her embroidery*) I don't like untidiness.

SIBYL. It wasn't like that, Mary. It was colour, and warmth, beauty and stillness. It was a lighter step and the sun on the river. Mary, I never lived till I met Christian—you can't refuse the gift of life.

LADY STARCROSS. Even if it's another woman's husband who offers it?

SIBYL. Do you think that marriage bars all other relationships—all other friendships?

LADY STARCROSS. Do you generally go to bed with your friends?

SIBYL. Christian said love was at its very best when it was friendship tinged with passion. He was my lover and my friend, and I was his.

(LADY STARCROSS *looks almost quizzically at Sibyl then puts the folded embroidery behind one of the sofa cushions*)

LADY STARCROSS. You've had your turn, Sibyl, now it's mine. Sit down. It's a very picturesque attitude, but sit down.

(SIBYL *sits abruptly in the tub chair*)

Women like you, Sibyl, for all your glamour and intelligence are apt to make a big mistake. You never realize what cards a wife holds in her hands.

SIBYL. Oh, but I do. You have all the aces—children, the ace of hearts—the joint banking account, the ace of diamonds—the back garden, the ace of spades. What chance has a woman with only love in her hand against you?

LADY STARCROSS. You've left out the ace of trumps, Sibyl—habit. Now Christian had a habit of coming every evening before he undressed and sitting on my bed and talking over everything that had happened during the day—including all the people he'd met—including you.

SIBYL. Me?

LADY STARCROSS. If I am cruel, please believe me that it's not because of what is past—it's because you mustn't waste the next twenty years of your life for a love that was never there.

SIBYL. What do you mean? I loved Christian. He loved me.

LADY STARCROSS. My dear, he was flattered. You were a very attractive young woman and you flung yourself at his head in a most engaging manner. He was only human. How could he resist you?

SIBYL. What are you trying to say, Mary?

LADY STARCROSS. We used to tease him about you. Poor Christian, how embarrassed he used to get. Don't think he wasn't fond of you, my dear, he was—very fond, but he was worried, too —he didn't want any trouble with Rickey. He was devoted to Rickey.

SIBYL. Are you trying to say he didn't love me?

LADY STARCROSS. He always said what fun you'd be to love— for someone else. How he hated it when you read poetry aloud to him—especially Swinburne!

SIBYL. He loved me.

LADY STARCROSS. Haven't I been cruel enough? Must I go on further before you'll realize anything. Must I underline everything, dot every I, cross every T?

SIBYL (*rising*) He loved me.

LADY STARCROSS. No, Sybil, he never loved you. He was attracted to you, but he never loved you. You made him laugh quite a lot, but he used to laugh at you quite a lot, too—oh, when will women realize what cats husbands are when the front door closes upon their dearest friends!

SIBYL. Nothing you say, Mary, can touch me. I am as sure of Christian's love as I am that the sun will rise again tomorrow.

LADY STARCROSS. You're not sure, Sibyl. In your heart you are frightened because you know that if he'd loved you he'd have written that last letter to you.

SIBYL. He wrote that last letter to the world through you. As you've kept on repeating you were his wife. I was only "the other woman". He couldn't write to me.

LADY STARCROSS. No-one has ever seen the original of the letter he wrote to me, Sibyl, except Ellen, who found it among the pages of the little copy of *Horace* he always carried with him, and myself—but you shall see it—and see the parts of it I never published to the world.

SIBYL. No!

LADY STARCROSS. Are you afraid? (*She rises and moves to the desk*)

SIBYL. I won't read it. You've no right to show it to me.

LADY STARCROSS (*taking a leather box from the desk*) It is mine— I can show it to whoever I choose.

SIBYL. He wouldn't have wished it.

LADY STARCROSS (*taking a faded letter from the box*) How do you know what he would have wished? (*She crosses with the letter to Sibyl*)
SIBYL (*crossing below the sofa to* R) I won't! I won't, I tell you.
LADY STARCROSS. Then I'll read it to you.
SIBYL. No! No, Mary.
LADY STARCROSS. I'll read it to you.
SIBYL. Mary, for pity's sake.
LADY STARCROSS. It's the last page. (*She reads*) "This, my last pillow of snow, is ever your breast and I lay me down gladly. 'Glad did I live and did gladly die.' Good old R.L.S. I must be wandering—I keep hearing snatches of those ragtime choruses we used to sing 'somewhere in France'. But if I've ever wandered I've come back to you now for ever.

(SIBYL *collapses in the easy chair*)

You are my habitation and my home, my resting place, my happy grave. Good night, my love. Good night, my mouse." (*She folds the letter and looks at Sibyl*)

(SIBYL, *utterly stricken, crouches in her chair*)

(*Gently*) It was written to me, Sibyl.
SIBYL (*in a strange little voice*) He called *me* his mouse.
LADY STARCROSS. Men are seldom very discriminating in their endearments. (*She crosses to the desk and replaces the letter*)

(SIBYL *begins to laugh highly and nervously like an hysterical child*)

SIBYL. How terribly funny, how terribly funny!
LADY STARCROSS. I'm afraid I don't see anything particularly amusing about it.
SIBYL (*rising*) But you're wrong, Mary—it's the funniest thing that ever happened.
LADY STARCROSS. Pull yourself together, Sibyl.
SIBYL (*crossing to the sofa*) He's tricked both of us—that's what's so funny.
LADY STARCROSS (*standing by the sofa*) You're hysterical. I'm sorry I had to tell you what I did, but it was the only way to make you understand.
SIBYL (*crossing to the fireplace*) A phoney lover and a phoney hero—you don't think that's funny?
LADY STARCROSS. What are you talking about?
SIBYL (*sitting in the tub chair*) He's tricked us—I thought he was in love with me and you thought he was a hero—and he wasn't either.
LADY STARCROSS (*crossing to Sibyl*) Sibyl, I know it's been a shock . . .
SIBYL. Shock? It's a joke. It's the best joke in the world on both of us.

LADY STARCROSS. Stop it, Sibyl—stop it.

SIBYL. What fools we've been. Wasting our lives like this—I on a bogus love and you on a bogus legend: you can't say it isn't the funniest thing that ever happened.

(CHRISTINE *enters. She is followed on by* TRENCHARD *and* PHILLIPS, *who are both wearing dinner jackets*)

CHRISTINE (*as she enters*) Mummy ... (*She looks at Sibyl and realizes they are intruding on some emotional crisis. She turns to go, indicating that Trenchard and Phillips should go with her*) I'm so sorry.

SIBYL (*rising quickly and moving down* C) Wait!

(CHRISTINE, TRENCHARD *and* PHILLIPS *pause in the open doorway, turn and look at Sibyl*)

You must share the joke, all of you—you can't miss the joke of the century. You're going to make a film about Christian—well, he was a fake.

LADY STARCROSS. Stop it, Sibyl! Stop it!

SIBYL. He was a fake, I tell you—it was all in Rickey's letter. Christian Starcross was a bloody fake!

She collapses in violent hysteria on the sofa as—

the CURTAIN *falls*

ACT III

Scene—*The same. The following morning.*

A large portrait of Christian Starcross now hangs above the mantelpiece. He has a small head and wide shoulders. The eyes are light, the chin pointed and the expression arrogant.

When the Curtain *rises* Ellen *stands at the open door, showing in* Trenchard *and* Phillips. Phillips *is in a state of agitation which he is trying hard to control, but* Trenchard *is his usual self.*

Trenchard. Wonderful morning, isn't it, Ellen?
Ellen (*grimly*) Aye.

(Ellen *exits, closing the door behind her*)

Trenchard (*moving towards the fireplace*) "Dour" is the word, I think. (*He notices the portrait*) Now that's interesting, very interesting. I wonder why?
Phillips (*irritably*) Why what?
Trenchard (*standing in front of the fireplace and looking up at the portrait*) Why now? Why put it there now? It's a gesture, obviously, but a gesture of what? Reassurance? Defiance?

(Phillips *shrugs and moves with his characteristic jerkiness to the window*)

It's an actor's face. It's the face of an actor playing a hero.
Phillips (*explosively*) This is one hell of a situation, isn't it?
Trenchard. Could be.
Phillips. Could be—it is.
Trenchard. We don't know yet, George. The woman may have been saying anything that came into her head. She's obviously an hysteric.
Phillips. All that about a letter from Rickey—was it the letter he left for her?
Trenchard. I suppose so. (*He pauses and gazes at the portrait*) I wonder if she's wise.
Phillips. Who?
Trenchard (*turning*) Lady Starcross. I wonder if it's wise to hold this—this post-mortem on Miss Emerson's hysterical outburst. I think I should simply have ignored it.
Phillips. She wanted to, but Christine wouldn't hear of it.
Trenchard. I see. Christine says in effect that Miss Emerson must either refute or substantiate her statement.

D

PHILLIPS. And quite right, too. Poor Christine! Poor darling, it's terrible for her.

TRENCHARD. I think I'm very glad I'm middle aged and don't want things in black and white like you young people.

PHILLIPS. She called him a fake.

TRENCHARD. A fake. I wonder . . . (*He turns and looks at the portrait*) A narrow head, pale blue eyes—killer's eyes. A good nose—a bit fleshy at the tip. Mouth small and rather disappointing—he has obviously tightened his lips to give it character. A chin that cries out for an Elizabethan ruff. Ugly hands.

PHILLIPS (*crossing, standing behind Trenchard and looking up at the portrait; surprised*) You can't see them.

TRENCHARD. If they'd been good we would have.

(*There is a silence*)

PHILLIPS (*moving above the sofa*) Damned unpunctual family this—always keeping us waiting. Jim, if—if something rotten does come out—I mean, if there's anything in what the Emerson woman said . . . (*He breaks off uncertainly*)

TRENCHARD. What'll happen about our picture?

(PHILLIPS *nods, moves and perches himself on the right arm of the sofa*)

(*He turns and paces above the sofa to the window*) You know, I've always been interested in this subject. I think it's a magnificent story and should be made at all costs, but there's one thing I haven't been interested in, and that's the man himself and his particular brand of courage. Nobility and what I believe is called "sheer courage" always rather bores me. Giants like Scott, Shackleton and the Everest boys leave me cold—they lack humanity somehow, or perhaps it's their trailing clouds of glory that obscure them for me. The average shelter marshal or ambulance driver in the blitz, the man dying cheerfully of an incurable disease—those are my sort of heroes—men who can't be bothered with achievement, men who'd rather stay in a nice warm bed—men who are human. Starcross has never been human to me. I hope we find he was vain and venal, unscrupulous and disastrous, that he hated discomfort, that he was afraid of the dark. Of course we shan't be able to show it on the screen, but we shall know he was real—not just a beautiful picture in a beautiful golden frame. Give me a cigarette.

PHILLIPS } (*together*) { You forgot to bring any.
TRENCHARD }   { I forgot to bring any.

PHILLIPS (*grinning*) You shouldn't get so carried away, Jim, it's bad for your ulcers. (*He takes a packet of cigarettes and a lighter from his pocket*)

TRENCHARD (*crossing to Phillips*) And I hope Starcross had ulcers, too.

(*They both laugh, but* PHILLIPS *stops abruptly. As he speaks,* TRENCHARD *takes a cigarette and* PHILLIPS *lights it for him*)

PHILLIPS. You know, I can't understand that woman—it wasn't as if she were drunk. What in the world did Lady Starcross do, or say, to get her into such a state? I never thought that she was the type of woman who would go off the deep end like that. From all the reports, and what the other women said, I gathered she was cool and calm, rather deep—certainly not one who would behave as she did last night.

TRENCHARD. You mean it was out of character?

PHILLIPS. I should have said so.

TRENCHARD. But people are always behaving "out of character". Driven on by sex, inferiority, unhappiness, ambition or simply by strain of some kind they do things, or say things that we, or they, don't know they are capable of. That is what makes life so fascinating, so exciting—and so surprising. And that is why the characters in most of our films are so unreal—they are all in one piece and we sweat blood to keep them like that. If *Hamlet* had come in to us as a film script by an unknown author, we'd have cut out everything he said or did as being out of character until there was no character left.

PHILLIPS. Jim, I think you're just talking to keep my mind off the subject in hand.

TRENCHARD (*crossing to the fireplace*) Quite right—clever of you to spot it.

PHILLIPS. Oh, it was quite in character.

(*They both laugh*)

TRENCHARD. You know, when two women hate each other as those two do, anything may happen. Funny thing, but in spite of last night, or maybe because of last night, this room has suddenly come alive. The air isn't so rarefied, it's easier to breathe.

PHILLIPS (*rising, crossing to* R. *of Trenchard and looking up at the portrait; moodily*) I suppose they must have had an affair—Sibyl and Starcross, I mean.

TRENCHARD (*curiously*) Why do you mind so much, George?

PHILLIPS. Dunno. Unsophisticated of me, isn't it. But the fact remains that I do.

TRENCHARD. It must be the Sir Galahad in you. You don't think Sibyl Emerson attractive?

PHILLIPS. I don't think anybody could have found her attractive last night.

TRENCHARD (*crossing and sitting on the sofa*) Possibly not. But I think you will find that the basic difference between the two women is that Lady Starcross—is charming, whereas Sibyl Emerson—has charm.

PHILLIPS (*standing with his back to the fire*) That's much too subtle a difference for a bloke like me.

TRENCHARD. Well, think of the women you know, the women to whom the world "charming" applies. Aren't they all a little too organized, too active, too over-bright? Don't they all make rather an effort and expect you to make rather an effort too? Now a woman who has charm doesn't need to make any effort at all. She is warmer, deeper, softer. In her company there is no sense of effort or strain. And when men turn to her they never turn away again. Men are invariably unfaithful to "charming" women, but a woman with charm can hold any man. Barrie called it "a sort of bloom on a woman". Well, Sibyl Emerson has a bloom upon her still. Forty, neurotic, hysterical but the bloom still works, the magic still holds. How unfair! How blazingly unfair. And the Communists affirm that all men were created equal—my God, if all women were, the world would be an easier place. Duller perhaps but . . .

(LADY STARCROSS *and* CHRISTINE *enter.* CHRISTINE *is in a nervous state, but* LADY STARCROSS *is quite controlled.* TRENCHARD *rises*)

LADY STARCROSS (*moving below the sofa*) How are you, Mr Trenchard? Good morning, George, I am glad you were both able to come.

TRENCHARD. Good morning, Lady Starcross.

PHILLIPS. Good morning, Lady Starcross.

CHRISTINE. Good morning, Mr Trenchard.

LADY STARCROSS. Miss Emerson won't be long. I suggest we sit down. (*She sits on the sofa*)

TRENCHARD (*crossing to* R) She is staying here? (*He sits in the easy chair*)

LADY STARCROSS. Yes—the doctor would not hear of her leaving last night. He gave her a sedative. She's very unwilling to meet you. However, Christine insists that she should give us an explanation of what she said last night.

TRENCHARD. Have you any idea what caused her outburst, Lady Starcross?

LADY STARCROSS. Yes, I'm afraid I caused it. As you heard so much, you might as well hear everything. You heard her speak of a bogus lover—well, Miss Emerson was very fond of my husband. He was attractive to, and attracted by, women—he was one of those men who found women's company stimulating—in fact he liked women. Very often this liking of his gave them the impression that he cared for them more deeply than was the case. I'm afraid Miss Emerson imagined he felt for her as deeply as she felt for him. She was what I believe is known as an "enthusiastic amateur", and my husband was—a normal man. I always knew it was because of her adoration of him that she retired from the world, but I hoped that she would recover and come back, and not go on wasting herself. Then last night I realized that as long as she thought she was the heroine of a great love, she would fritter away the rest of her life as she had frittered away the last twenty years. So, mistakenly or not, I told her that my husband had never loved her—and that was what caused the outburst. She wanted to hit back. It was very understandable. I don't know whether I was right in being so drastic, but I hate waste, and Sibyl's an intelligent woman who should be giving something to the world. I found her difficult to convince, so I read her part of my husband's last letter to me.

TRENCHARD. I see, you cauterized the wound with a hot poker.

(LADY STARCROSS, *sensing an undercurrent in Trenchard's tone, gives him a sharp look*)

LADY STARCROSS. Yes, it's kinder in the end—kinder and quicker.

TRENCHARD. I see now why the first time we came here you told us that Miss Emerson cheapened everything she touched.

CHRISTINE (*moving to Trenchard*) Well, mother was right, wasn't she? She tried to cheapen my father.

LADY STARCROSS (*to Trenchard*) I suppose you tried to find some reason for my saying that—some personal motive?

TRENCHARD. Yes. We were unsuccessful.

LADY STARCROSS. I'm afraid this is all going to be very embarrassing.

CHRISTINE. What does that matter? Sibyl Emerson slandered my father in front of you and George. She said he was a fake.

TRENCHARD. She was in a state. You've heard what your mother said. People say anything when they're in a state like that.

CHRISTINE. She said Rickey knew he was a fake, too.

TRENCHARD. Rickey was probably very jealous of her feeling for your father.

CHRISTINE. I don't care. He was my father—no-one's going to say things like that against my father and get away with it—and certainly not a vile woman like that.

PHILLIPS. Christine!

CHRISTINE. Well, she *is* vile.

PHILLIPS. Oh come, Christine, you can't . . .

CHRISTINE. She had an affair with him, didn't she?

TRENCHARD. But, Miss Starcross . . .

CHRISTINE. Oh, I suppose you pride yourself on being tolerant.

TRENCHARD. I don't pride myself on anything, Miss Starcross. But I do try to be tolerant.

CHRISTINE. I believe in loyalty.

TRENCHARD. Aren't you confusing fidelity with loyalty?

D*

CHRISTINE. Aren't they the same thing?

TRENCHARD. No. Some of the most loyal men I know are unfaithful. And some of the most faithful are flagrantly disloyal.

CHRISTINE (*turning suddenly on Trenchard*) I suppose it means nothing to you in the film business, and I'm sure you must think me horribly old-fashioned—(*she moves up* C *and turns*) but I still think that a woman who runs after a married man is vile.

TRENCHARD (*smiling*) I'm afraid you'll find that there are a lot of vile people in the world, Miss Starcross. People who don't regard other people as pieces of property. Nobody belongs to anybody unless they want to.

PHILLIPS (*irritably*) Oh, come off it, Jim! This isn't the time to split hairs or words. Lady Starcross, there isn't a grain of truth in what she said, is there? I mean, there can't be, can there? She did get a letter from Rickey, I suppose?

LADY STARCROSS. Oh, yes, she did get a letter from Rickey.

(SIBYL *enters. She is very pale and very controlled. She is drained of all emotion. She does not smile but looks gravely at each of them in turn. She carries her coat*)

TRENCHARD (*rising*) Good morning, Miss Emerson.

LADY STARCROSS (*rising*) I'm glad you're better, Sibyl. (*She indicates the sofa*) Please come and sit down.

SIBYL (*crossing to the sofa*) Thank you. (*She puts her coat over the back of the sofa, then sits*)

(*There is a silence as* LADY STARCROSS *moves and stands below the wing chair*)

TRENCHARD (*impulsively*) Miss Emerson, if it's going to upset you in any way I, for one, have no desire to know what . . .

CHRISTINE (*crossing quickly to* L *of the sofa and interrupting*) Well, I have. (*She turns to Sibyl*) What did you mean last night about my father?

SIBYL (*to Lady Starcross; appealingly*) Mary—I can't—you must understand—I can't . . .

CHRISTINE. Shall I repeat to you what you said?

SIBYL (*wearily*) No. I remember it all.

CHRISTINE. Well?

SIBYL. Christine, please regard it all as the ravings of a stupid hysterical woman—a jealous woman—an insanely jealous woman.

CHRISTINE. What was in Rickey's letter about my father?

SIBYL. Oh—wild extravagant things—he must have been light-headed—it was all crazy—didn't make sense.

CHRISTINE. You're lying!

LADY STARCROSS. Christine!

CHRISTINE. I'm sorry, but you are lying, aren't you?

SIBYL. Yes. Listen, Christine, until last night I felt as passionately as you do about the truth—I thought the truth was all—

important, all-enduring—now I know that if happiness depended on a lie I'd welcome the lie for the happiness.

CHRISTINE (*inexorably*) I want to know why you said those things about my father—were they all lies?

SIBYL (*eagerly*) Yes, all of them. Just a mass of stupid neurotic nonsense—lies, all of them.

(SIBYL's *eyes fall before* CHRISTINE's *accusing face*)

TRENCHARD. Forgive me, Miss Emerson, but I think this has gone so far that it must go all the way. If there is anything you should tell Christine or Lady Starcross—and I think there must be—George and I will leave you.

CHRISTINE. No. We all heard it then—we must all hear it now.

(TRENCHARD *sits in the easy chair*)

SIBYL. Mary—say something. Help me—help yourself.

LADY STARCROSS (*sitting in the wing chair*) I agree with Mr Trenchard—we've reached the point of no return.

SIBYL (*slowly*) The point of no return—as they did. (*She buries her face in her hands, and then looks up and pushes her hair back from her forehead*)

(PHILLIPS *sits in the tub chair*)

You can only speak of people as you know them—as they appear to you. I can only speak of the Christian Starcross I knew—knew and loved—and he was the vainest man that ever drew breath.

(CHRISTINE *recoils*)

(*She smiles rather sadly at* CHRISTINE) The point of no return, Christine—I must go on. Christian's ego was colossal, but so well covered up with charm and intelligence and glamour—yes, glamour—the real thing, not the Hollywood version—that very few people suspected it. But he would do anything—anything—to blazon his name to the world—the name that wasn't his name. (*She looks at Lady Starcross*)

(LADY STARCROSS *looks steadily at Sibyl*)

CHRISTINE. What do you mean?

SIBYL (*looking at Lady Starcross*) His name was Leonard Williamson.

CHRISTINE (*turning to Lady Starcross*) Mother . . . ?

LADY STARCROSS (*quietly*) Yes, it's quite true, darling. He changed it by deed poll.

CHRISTINE. But why? Why did he . . . ?

SIBYL. Take a "stage name"?

CHRISTINE (*turning to Sibyl*) Yes. He wasn't an actor.
SIBYL. No.
LADY STARCROSS. He saw Starcross on a railway station in Devon when he was a boy. He always remembered it.
PHILLIPS (*slowly*) Leonard Williamson.
SIBYL (*rising*) Yes, it doesn't fit the role, does it? (*She pauses*) Must I go on? What good can it do? I've caused enough misery. Christine, have pity and let me go. Have pity on me, on your mother, on all of us. Pretend this never happened.
CHRISTINE. But it has happened. Don't you see, I must know. I can't go on as I did before, I'd never have any peace. I'd always be imagining. . . . If there's anything to know, I must know it.
SIBYL (*moving* RC) Very well, Christine, I'll tell you. Christian was one of those people to whom anything is preferable to the monotony of everyday life, so quite naturally he enjoyed the nineteen-fourteen—nineteen-eighteen war. He won the M.C. and was recommended for the V.C.—but he didn't get it as he often risked the lives of his men quite unnecessarily—oh yes, he did, Mary, John Halliday was one of them. Well, when the war ended he came back into the world in which he had no place, a world that didn't turn its head each time he passed by. A world too tired, too busy and too ill for heroes. He was desperate—where was he to find the only things he cared for, power and glory? And a chance meeting with Fred Shipman showed him. Fred had been on an early expedition with Scott. He fell at once for Christian and they went off to the far North together. Fred brought back a valuable treatise on respiration in those latitudes, and Christian the famous series of articles he called *Signs of Life Beyond the Abyss*. Oh yes, I'm telling you something you all know—but what you don't know is that Christian's articles were a brilliant fake.
CHRISTINE. No!
PHILLIPS (*rising*) It's impossible—why, they're classics.
SIBYL. Those "signs of life"—those abominable snowmen, those footprints on the ice—destroyed before his return by a convenient avalanche, never existed except in Christian's imagination. He said that de Rougement, Mandeville and Munchausen had nothing on him and he was proud of it.
LADY STARCROSS. He was making a fool of you.
SIBYL (*with sad dignity*) No, Mary, he made a fool of me over something else. This is all quite true and I thought it as amusing as he did at the time.
TRENCHARD (*rising*) Lady Starcross, I think if you don't mind . . .
SIBYL. Don't you believe me?
TRENCHARD (*gravely*) Yes, Miss Emerson, I believe you.
SIBYL. I'm going on, Mr Trenchard. I'm going to tell you why

I tried to stop you making this picture—I must, now. (*She pauses and looks at Trenchard*)

(TRENCHARD *inclines his head, and resumes his seat in the easy chair*)

Christian's aim on that last Expedition was quite clear—to Christian. I can see him now that last time he came to my flat. He was standing looking down at the river—with his head thrown up and his hands clasped behind his back, teetering a little on his heels—you know, Mary, how he used to . . . (*She checks herself abruptly. After a pause*) Suddenly he swung round. He was quite white and his eyes were blazing, and he said, "This will make me immortal—and I must have immortality—I will have immortality."

TRENCHARD. Poor devil!

(PHILLIPS *resumes his seat in the tub chair*)

SIBYL (*after a grateful glance at Trenchard*) And then his mood changed, he was like quicksilver—that was part of his excitement, those sudden changes of his—and he laughed. He laughed till he cried, till he choked and I had to thump him on the back and give him a glass of water. I asked him why he laughed and he said, "Because I've fooled old Garforth so beautifully." He had no evidence of the city—it was just a travellers' tale—but he wished to believe in it and therefore felt quite justified in faking evidence to convince old Garforth. There was no dying Lama.

PHILLIPS. But the golden emblem?

SIBYL. He'd bought that in a bazaar in Kashmir years ago.

CHRISTINE. That's not true!

SIBYL. I'm afraid it's perfectly true—but the travellers' tales weren't—I know that from Rickey's letter—there was no city.

CHRISTINE. But they saw it. It was in the log-book that they'd seen it. Father, Rickey and Dr Mowbray.

SIBYL (*sadly*) The log-book lied, Christine. Your father described something that wasn't there.

PHILLIPS (*quoting*) "The City of Tchu San Lei hanging like a cloud above dark space where the waters sang unseen. The cold sun glinted on a scarlet pinnacle. How many miles away? How many pitiless miles away?"

SIBYL. Yes, I like to think he saw it—even if only in his imagination.

TRENCHARD. Had the city ever existed?

SIBYL. I don't know. I don't think he knew. But being Christian it was enough for him that he wished for it to exist. If he wished to find the city it was unthinkable from his point of view that the city was not there waiting to be found. And being Christian he was able to convince the others, too.

CHRISTINE. But that means he led five men to certain death.

SIBYL. He believed in his stars, in his luck, in Christian Starcross, and they believed in it, too—and in him. (*She moves to the sofa and sits*)

(CHRISTINE *turns and looks silently at Phillips*)

LADY STARCROSS. Is this all you have to say?
SIBYL. Not quite. (*With a touch of bitterness*) I haven't Rickey's last letter with me, but I know it by heart. (*She looks around hoping that she will not have to go on with the story*)

(CHRISTINE, *with agonized eyes, stares unwinkingly at Sibyl.* LADY STARCROSS *might be carved out of stone*)

(*She gives a little shrug, then continues with an expressionless voice, her eyes staring into vacancy*) This was written a few hours before the rifle went off—accidentally. Rickey said, "I think we are in hell, my darling, and have been for many days. I hold out both hands to death longing for him to take me somewhere where Christian cannot follow me. I think he is the devil. Today he has told me many things—that he had no real evidence of the existence of the city of Tchu San Lei, that he could have saved Halliday and didn't, because John thought it was still possible to return, and he, Christian Starcross, would never turn back. He is completely mad, of course, and one wonders how long he's been like this. And I thought him a genius, a leader, a hero. There was never any hope for any of us. I am alone in these icy wastes with a madman. He boasts now because he knows it is safe to do so, and it must be a relief for him to be able to blow the whole sham skyhigh, and laugh and laugh. He says his name will live for evermore. I'm getting very weak but his strength is superhuman. He looked at me today and said, 'Why don't you do an Oates on me? Don't expect me to carry you if you fall.' I think he will kill me before long and I shall be grateful. He wants to be alone with his immortality . . ." (*She pauses*) There's very little more. "I don't know what will be said about us hereafter. His preparations were grossly inadequate. He was warned about the season, and he knew about Dan's heart. His insane vanity is utterly and completely to blame for every death and every disaster that has overtaken us, the man has murder and heartbreak on his soul, and yet as I look at him, sitting writing by the light of our last candle, there is something so gallant about the way he holds his head, that even now I cannot . . ." (*Simply*) That's the end of the letter—I think the candle went out.

(CHRISTINE *collapses* L *of Sibyl on the sofa. There is a long silence*)

LADY STARCROSS (*slowly*) "Something so gallant about the way he holds his head . . ."

(LADY STARCROSS *rises as if in a dream, crosses and exits. There is a pause, then* SIBYL *looks vaguely around, rises, picks up her coat and puts it over her arm.* CHRISTINE *stirs and looks up at Sibyl*)

SIBYL (*looking gravely at Christine*) Don't love him any the less, Christine, because he wasn't what you thought him. I don't love him the less because he never loved me.
CHRISTINE (*brokenly*) But everything's gone.
SIBYL. Yes. (*She moves to the door*)

(TRENCHARD *and* PHILLIPS *rise*)

TRENCHARD (*moving to the door*) Miss Emerson, can I drop you anywhere? I've got a car—I . . .

(SIBYL *exits, closing the door behind her.* PHILLIPS *crosses to Christine*)

(*He crosses to the fireplace. Slowly*) All these years, knowing the real story, all these years with only his love to make it bearable—a love that was never there.
PHILLIPS. What'll happen to her?
TRENCHARD. Nothing—there's nothing left to happen.

(ELLEN, *in a flurry, enters and crosses above the sofa to* L *of the left end*)

ELLEN. What's going on? Her ladyship locked in her room, and that woman walking out of the house like a ghost. Film people! We were all right till we got caught up with film people and that woman came here again. (*She pulls at Christine's arm and sees her tear-stained face*) Tears! Tears and that woman, and her ladyship locked in her room. Go up and wash that face, miss. Go on! This instant. (*She pulls* CHRISTINE *to her feet and pushes her towards the door*)

(PHILLIPS *makes a movement, but* ELLEN'S *look quells him*)

There! Go along now.

(ELLEN *leads* CHRISTINE *from the room.* PHILLIPS *crosses to the table* L *of the door, pours out a drink, swallows it in one gulp, then refills the glass and crosses with it to Trenchard.* TRENCHARD *takes the glass and as he drinks* ELLEN *re-enters. She gives a horrified look at* TRENCHARD, *who chokes and splutters so that* PHILLIPS *has to thump him on the back*)

(*Grimly*) Her ladyship says to wait for her and for coffee. But no doubt you'd be wanting something stronger.

(ELLEN *exits, slamming the door behind her*)

TRENCHARD (*crossing and sitting on the sofa*) Oh, my lord! Well, this has opened a can of peas and no mistake.
PHILLIPS. Poor kid. God, it's awful for her.

TRENCHARD. Yes—and not only for her.

(*There is a pause*)

PHILLIPS. Well, this is the end of the picture, Jim.
TRENCHARD. Give me a cigarette. Why is it the end of the picture?
PHILLIPS (*offering a cigarette to Trenchard*) D'you think I'm going to perpetuate this ghastly farce?
TRENCHARD (*taking a cigarette*) Why not? I don't see why it shouldn't be made—it's still a good story even if it isn't true—and who knows the real truth of any legend?

(PHILLIPS *lights Trenchard's cigarette*)

Are we so certain we know the truth about Christ? All that matters is the way of life known as Christianity.
PHILLIPS. If you learnt that Christ was a fake, you'd let the world go on believing in Him?
TRENCHARD. I would.
PHILLIPS. You're what's erroneously known as a Jesuit—you believe that the end justifies the means.
TRENCHARD. I'm also a gardener. I believe that the scent of roses justifies the stench of manure.
PHILLIPS (*moving down* L) I'm not making the picture, Jim. You'd better tell her. I'm not making it.

(LADY STARCROSS *and* CHRISTINE *enter.* LADY STARCROSS *seems to have re-charged herself.* CHRISTINE *has washed her face and seems calmer.* TRENCHARD *rises*)

LADY STARCROSS (*crossing to the window*) I told Ellen to bring coffee. Mr Trenchard, there are four of us here today who heard Sibyl Emerson's story. It must go no further.
TRENCHARD (*moving above the sofa*) You have my word.
LADY STARCROSS (*sitting in the easy chair*). Thank you.
CHRISTINE (*moving to the window*) But it must go further. We can't go on cheating the world like this—letting them believe in something which is false—in someone who . . .
TRENCHARD. Why not?
CHRISTINE. Why not? Because it is not true.
TRENCHARD. As a well-known proconsul once remarked— "What is Truth?" Wouldn't the truth in this case do infinite harm?
CHRISTINE (*turning*) Mr Trenchard, you don't begin to understand how I feel.
TRENCHARD. I think I do, and believe me I am most desperately sorry for you.
CHRISTINE. Thank you for being sorry, but you still don't understand.

PHILLIPS. I think I do. I think I'd feel the same.

(CHRISTINE *crosses to* R *of Phillips*)

I think you must tell the truth or you will hate yourself for ever. If you go through your life surrounded by people who believe that your father was a hero and say to you, as we said—"What's it like to be his daughter", and you answer, as you'll have to answer, "Wonderful", you will feel deathly sick and deathly ashamed. You'll be perpetually achieving people's interest and compassion by false pretences, by being something that you are not.

CHRISTINE. Thank you, George—you do understand.
PHILLIPS. Perhaps it's because I understand you.
CHRISTINE. Yes.

(*There is a silence*)

PHILLIPS (*crossing to* L *of Lady Starcross*) I am not going to make the film, Lady Starcross. I can't.

LADY STARCROSS. I'm sorry, George. What about you, Mr Trenchard?

TRENCHARD. I see no reason for changing my plans.

PHILLIPS (*turning to Trenchard*) You can see no reason! My God!

TRENCHARD. There are millions of people in the world, George, who are born hero-worshippers. To those people, Christian Starcross—the man and his story—are a help and an inspiration. They were to you. In his life and his death he gave them an ideal to live up to, a destination to set out for. We live in a time of fear, disillusionment and man's unhumanity to man. Everywhere there is cynicism, frustration, lack of belief. It is the Age of Despair. I will not add to this despair by destroying the Starcross Legend, which, true or false, I consider a power for good—constructive good. I'm going to make this picture. I'm going to make every man and every boy feel that there is still something big beyond our shrinking horizons. If I denied people this because of squaring my own measly conscience, or satisfying my own piddling passion for truth, I should despise myself for the rest of my life.

LADY STARCROSS. Thank you, Mr Trenchard.
TRENCHARD. Well, George?
PHILLIPS. I won't make it. I can't.
CHRISTINE. I'm very glad.
TRENCHARD. And I'm very sorry. I'll have to get someone else.
PHILLIPS. You can't make it.
CHRISTINE. But everyone will know the story's false.
TRENCHARD. Why? Are you going to tell them?
CHRISTINE. Yes.
TRENCHARD. How? Call a "press conference"?

CHRISTINE. Why not?

TRENCHARD (*gently*) What a little exhibitionist you are.

PHILLIPS. Jim!

CHRISTINE. I don't care what you call me, I'm not going to live in this atmosphere of fakes and lies any longer.

PHILLIPS. She's quite right.

LADY STARCROSS. She's quite wrong. (*She rises and crosses to Christine*) You stupid child! You are trying to take out your own unhappiness on the world. You're selfish and vain—like your father.

CHRISTINE. Mother!

LADY STARCROSS. Not once have you given a thought to me, not once! How do you think I shall feel when you have your press conference? When I see everything I have fought for tumbling in ruins about me? I have fought for your father's immortality because he wished to be immortal—I knew his ambitions quite as well as that woman did—and it doesn't matter to me if that immortality is true or false. What matters to me—is that he wanted it. I shall not allow you to diminish his stature by the fraction of an inch.

TRENCHARD (*softly*) Bravo!

LADY STARCROSS. And I will not have you inform the gentlemen of the press that your father was unfaithful to me with the fiancée of his best friend.

CHRISTINE. Mother—I wasn't going to say anything about that.

LADY STARCROSS. Why not? It's the truth. Why keep anything back?

PHILLIPS. Lady Starcross—please.

LADY STARCROSS. What a puny, queasy generation you are—full of half-baked ideals, without the courage to lie for those you love. What an unreticent gutless generation! You'll never be the men and women your parents were. You're milk, water, uniform, spirit-less. (*She pauses*) If you had any spirit, George, you'd make this picture the finest you've worked on, but you haven't any spirit. No, I expect you describe yourself as having "integrity", which nowadays seems to cover a multitude of negatives.

CHRISTINE. Mother, I didn't realize—I thought you'd feel the way I did.

LADY STARCROSS. Why? How could there be any similarity in our feelings? I loved your father. When he died I died, too, but I had to pretend to go on living. You were too young to be a companion to me, but I had his Legend to comfort my loneliness, and with the years it grew and grew and will last as long as humanity exists upon this earth.

TRENCHARD (*softly*)
"As long as men can breathe, or eyes can see,
So long lives this, and this gives life to thee."

LADY STARCROSS. Please God . . .

(CHRISTINE *flings herself weeping into her mother's arms*)

CHRISTINE. Oh, Mummy, Mummy, forgive me.

PHILLIP (*uncomfortably*) Well—er—I think I must be getting along.

LADY STARCROSS. Christine, darling, pull yourself together and show George out, and then I suggest a good hot bath and lunch in bed.

CHRISTINE. Oh, Mummy!

(LADY STARCROSS *disengages herself*)

LADY STARCROSS (*crossing to Phillips*) Good-bye, George. I'm sorry it won't be you on the picture.

PHILLIPS. So am I. Good-bye, Lady Starcross, and thank you.

LADY STARCROSS. What for? For telling you you come of a gutless generation?

PHILLIPS. Possibly. (*He moves to the door*) Coming, Jim?

TRENCHARD. Not this minute.

(PHILLIPS *holds out his hand to* CHRISTINE, *who crosses to him.* PHILLIPS *and* CHRISTINE *exit together*)

LADY STARCROSS (*turning to Trenchard with a little helpless gesture*) Was I too hard?

TRENCHARD (*moving to L of Lady Starcross*) No.

LADY STARCROSS. Poor Christine.

TRENCHARD. Youth is blessedly resilient. There's little that can't be miraculously helped by a hot bath and a great many telephone calls from George Phillips.

LADY STARCROSS. I like you, Mr Trenchard. I think we understand each other.

TRENCHARD. I think I understand you well enough to know how completely unimportant Miss Emerson's revelations were to you today. It was almost as if they were no surprise to you.

LADY STARCROSS. I don't really think they were. I suppose I've always known subconsciously that the Expedition must have been his biggest bluff of all. (*She looks up at the portrait*) Poor darling. Poor darling.

TRENCHARD. He was much loved by two very remarkable women.

LADY STARCROSS. It was like loving the sunshine. You don't question the moral character of the sunshine—you just thank God for it. (*She crosses to the fireplace and gazes up at the portrait*)

TRENCHARD (*looking up at the portrait*) Is it a good portrait of him?

LADY STARCROSS. Yes, it's very like.

TRENCHARD. I wondered why . . . ?

LADY STARCROSS. Why I put it up today?

TRENCHARD. Yes.

LADY STARCROSS. For many years I couldn't bear to look at it, but today, for some reason, I felt strong enough. It will hang there always now.

TRENCHARD (*moving below the sofa; softly*) Good-bye.

(LADY STARCROSS, *looking up at the portrait, does not seem to hear him.*

TRENCHARD *turns and exits, almost colliding with* ELLEN, *who enters at the same moment. She carries a tray of coffee for one, which she puts on the table* L *of the door*)

ELLEN (*pouring the coffee*) They've all gone?

LADY STARCROSS (*turning, moving to the sofa and perching herself on the left arm of it*) Yes.

ELLEN. *She* walked out of the house like she was walking into her grave.

LADY STARCROSS. Who?

ELLEN. Sibyl Emerson.

LADY STARCROSS. Yes.

ELLEN (*handing a cup of coffee to Lady Starcross*) The portrait looks fine.

LADY STARCROSS. Yes, I no longer mind that he was in love with her when it was painted—that his eyes were full of the reflection of hers. Because she's got nothing now. I've taken everything back—everything she ever took from me.

ELLEN. Och, the master was daft! What could he ever see in her?

LADY STARCROSS. She touched his imagination, Ellen, and when a woman does that a man loves her all the days of his life, and when he's dying writes her a deathless letter.

ELLEN. I've always been afraid she'd find out that he wrote that letter to her.

LADY STARCROSS. Found out it was hers? How could she after all these years? You burnt the envelope yourself, didn't you?

ELLEN. Aye.

LADY STARCROSS. No, she'll never know now that in the end he came back to her for ever.

ELLEN. Drink up your coffee—it's getting cold.

Still looking at the arrogant painted face above the mantelpiece, LADY STARCROSS *raises the cup to her lips as—*

the CURTAIN *falls*

FURNITURE AND PROPERTY PLOT

ACT I

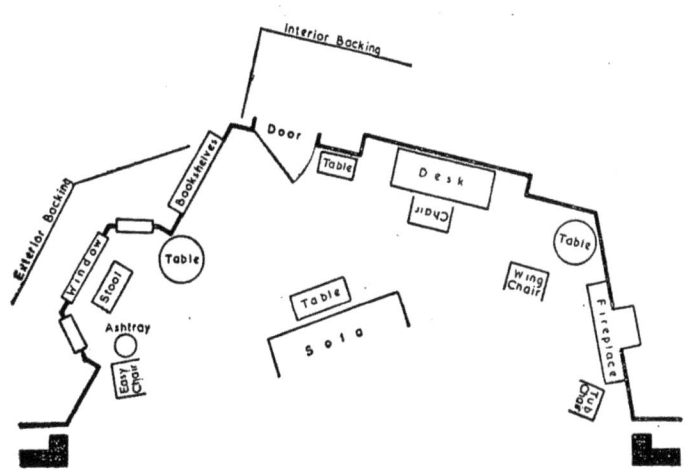

On stage: Easy chair. *On it:* cushion
Stool
Pedestal ashtray
Occasional table. *On it:* table lamp, bowl of flowers, ashtray, ornament
Built-in bookshelves. *On them:* books, ornaments
Small table (L of door) *On it:* decanter of sherry, jug of water, 6 sherry glasses, ornament
Table (C) *On it:* ashtray, box with cigarettes
Sofa. *On it:* cushions, film script
Writing desk. *On it:* vase of flowers, table-lamp, inkstand, blotter, pen, stationery, ashtray
  In drawer: leather box with letter, embroidery with silk and needle
Wing chair. *On it:* cushion
Circular table. *On it:* vase of flowers, ornament, ashtray
On mantelpiece: ornaments, small mirror
Over mantelpiece: mirror
Pair fire-dogs

Fire-irons
Hearth rug
Tub chair. *On it:* cushion
Net curtains for window
Heavy curtains and pelmet
Carpet on floor
Light switch L of door
Bell-push
Pictures on walls
Pair electric candle-lamp wall-brackets

Off stage: Tea trolley. *On it:* cloth, 4 each cups, saucers, teaspoons, plates, knives. Pot with tea, jug with milk, basin with sugar, plate of scones, plate of cakes (ELLEN)
Dish of jam (ELLEN)
Tray. *On it:* decanter of gin, bottle of French vermouth, decanter of sherry (ELLEN)
Large envelope with photographs (CHRISTINE)
Large envelope with legal document (LADY STARCROSS)

Personal: CHLOE: handbag. *In it:* matches
TRENCHARD: watch
PHILLIPS: packet of cigarettes

Window curtains open
Door shut
Fire lit
Lights out

ACT II

Off stage: Telephone on long lead (CHRISTINE)

Personal: CHRISTINE: watch, evening bag. *In it:* cosmetics
SIBYL: cigarette

Window open
Window curtains open
Door shut
Fire lit
Desk lamp lit
Other lights out

During CURTAIN fall:

Set below sofa:

Tea trolley. *On it:* 5 each coffee-cups, saucers, spoons, pot with coffee, jug with milk, basin with sugar

ACT III

Strike: Mirror over mantelpiece

Set: *Over mantelpiece:* portrait of Christian Starcross

Off stage: Tray. *On it:* cup, saucer, spoon, pot with coffee, basin with sugar, jug with milk (ELLEN)

Personal: PHILLIPS: packet of cigarettes, lighter

Window curtains open
Fire lit
Door open
Lights out

LIGHTING PLOT

Propety fittings required:
> Fire in grate, practical
> 2 table lamps, practical
> 2 pairs electric candle-lamp wall-brackets, practical
> Light switch L of door
> Bell push above fireplace

Interior. The same scene throughout

ACT I

Late afternoon. April

The Apparent Souce of Light is daylight through the window
If practicable, a reflected ripple effect presumed to come from the river should show on the tops of the walls and ceiling

> *To open.* All lights full up
> Fire lit
> Table-lamps and brackets out

> Cue 1. LADY STARCROSS opens window (Page 14)
> Commence slow dim as dusk falls
> Switch off ripple effect

> Cue 2. LADY STARCROSS switches on wall-brackets (Page 15)
> Bring up lights

ACT II

Early evening

> *To open.* Dusk outside window
> Fire lit
> Desk lamp lit
> Other lamps out

> Cue 1. CHRISTINE switches on wall-brackets (Page 21)
> Switch on wall-brackets
> Bring up lights

ACT III

Morning

To open. Sunshine outside window
All lights full up
Fire lit
Table lamps and brackets out

No cues

Milton Keynes UK
Ingram Content Group UK Ltd.
UKHW021911220424
441566UK00027B/370